Skewered Delights

Flavorful Beef BBQ and Grilled Kabobs

The Golden Plate Fuus

Contents

INTRODUCTION

Are you ready for a culinary adventure? Skewered Delights: 98 Flavorful Beef BBQ and Grilled Kabobs will take you on a journey of tantalizing flavors, succulent meats, and mouthwatering spices. This cookbook is perfect for anyone who loves grilling and barbecuing, and is looking for new and exciting recipes to try.

Kabobs have been around for centuries, and it's not hard to see why. They are a delicious and easy way to cook meat, vegetables, and fruits, and the possibilities are endless. Whether you're looking for a quick and easy weeknight meal, or planning a backyard barbecue with friends and family, kabobs are the perfect choice.

Skewered Delights offers a wide range of recipes, from classic beef kabobs to more exotic flavors like Korean beef bulgogi and Middle Eastern shish kabobs. Each recipe has been carefully crafted to ensure you get the best possible results, and is accompanied by beautiful photographs to inspire and guide you as you cook.

One of the great things about kabobs is that they are so versatile. You can mix and match meats, vegetables, and spices to create your own unique combinations. Skewered Delights provides plenty of inspiration, with recipes like beef and mushroom kabobs, teriyaki beef and pineapple kabobs, and Greek-style beef and tomato skewers.

Of course, no kabob cookbook would be complete without some delicious marinades and sauces. Skewered Delights has plenty to choose from, including a classic teriyaki sauce, a spicy Thai chili sauce, and a tangy yogurt and herb marinade. These sauces and marinades will take your kabobs to the next level, infusing them with even more flavor and complexity.

In addition to beef kabobs, Skewered Delights also includes recipes for chicken, shrimp, and vegetable kabobs. This makes it a great choice for anyone who wants to cater to different tastes and dietary requirements. Whether you're a meat-lover or a vegetarian, there's something here for everyone.

Another great thing about kabobs is that they are a healthy and nutritious meal option. By incorporating lots of fresh vegetables and lean meats, you can create a balanced meal that is both delicious and good for you. Skewered Delights takes this into account, and provides plenty of tips and tricks for cooking healthy and flavorful kabobs.

In conclusion, Skewered Delights: 98 Flavorful Beef BBQ and Grilled Kabobs is the ultimate cookbook for anyone who loves grilling and barbecuing. It offers a wide range of recipes, from classic beef kabobs to more exotic flavors, and provides plenty of inspiration for mixing and matching ingredients. With beautiful photographs and easy-to-follow instructions, this cookbook will soon become your go-to guide for all things kabob-related. So fire up the grill, gather your friends and family, and get ready to enjoy some delicious skewered delights!

1. Classic Beef Skewers with Vegetables

This classic recipe for beef skewers with vegetables is a tasty dinner or entertainment option that everyone will enjoy! It is full of flavor, with juicy pieces of beef and vegetables marinated in a savory mixture and served with a zesty yogurt dipping sauce.

Serving: This recipe serves 6-8.

Preparation Time: 15 minutes

Ready Time: 30 minutes (including marinating time)

Ingredients:
- 2 pounds beef sirloin, cut into 2-inch cubes
- 2 bell peppers, cut into 2-inch cubes
- 1 large onion, cut into 2-inch cubes
- 1 zucchini, cut into 2-inch cubes
- 3 cloves garlic, grated
- 3 tablespoons olive oil
- 1 teaspoon sea salt
- 1 teaspoon black pepper
- 2 tablespoons Worcestershire sauce
- 3 tablespoons tomato paste
- 2 tablespoons fresh parsley

Instructions:
1. Mix together garlic, oil, salt, pepper, Worcestershire sauce, tomato paste and parsley in a large bowl.
2. Add beef, bell peppers, onion, and zucchini to the bowl and mix together to combine.
3. Cover and refrigerate for 1 hour.
4. Preheat the grill on medium-high heat.
5. Skewer the marinated beef and vegetables onto the skewers.
6. Grill for 6-7 minutes per side or until the beef is at the desired doneness.
7. Serve with a yogurt dipping sauce.

Nutrition Information:
Serving size: 1 skewer
Calories: 250

Total Fat: 16g
Saturated Fat: 5g
Cholesterol: 65mg
Sodium: 450mg
Total Carbohydrate: 6g
Dietary Fiber: 1g
Protein: 22g

2. Beef and Mushroom Skewers

Beef and Mushroom Skewers – A delightful combination of marinated beef and mushrooms, these skewers are perfect for any occasion!
Serving: 6
Preparation Time: 15 minutes
Ready Time: 30 minutes

Ingredients:
• 1 lb. of beef cubes
• 12-14 mushrooms of any variety
• 2 tablespoons of olive oil
• 2 tablespoons of Worcestershire sauce
• 2 tablespoons of soy sauce
• 2 tablespoons of honey
• 2 teaspoons of garlic powder
• Salt and black pepper to taste

Instructions:
1. In a medium bowl, mix together the olive oil, Worcestershire sauce, soy sauce, honey, garlic powder, salt and pepper.
2. Add the beef cubes and mushrooms to the marinade and mix together until all the Ingredients are evenly coated.
3. Preheat the oven to 375°F.
4. Skewer the beef cubes and mushrooms onto metal or wooden skewers.
5. Place the skewers onto a baking sheet covered with parchment paper.
6. Bake in the preheated oven for about 30 minutes until the beef is cooked through.
7. Remove from the oven and serve.

Nutrition Information:
Per Serving: Calories: 195 kcal
Carbohydrates: 7 g
Protein: 23 g
Fat: 8 g
Saturated Fat: 2 g
Cholesterol: 48 mg
Sodium: 316 mg
Potassium: 330 mg
Fiber: 1 g
Sugar: 4 g

3. Teriyaki Beef Skewers

These teriyaki beef skewers are a delicious and savory Asian-inspired dish that your whole family will love. This flavorful marinade tastes great on all kinds of meats and vegetables and pairs wonderfully with steamed/fried rice or noodles.
Servings: 4
Preparation Time: 20 minutes
Ready Time: 1 hour

Ingredients:
- 1.5 lbs of boneless beef short ribs, cubed
- 2/3 cup soy sauce
- 1/2 cup brown sugar
- 2 garlic cloves, finely minced
- 2 tablespoons grated fresh ginger
- 2 tablespoons sesame oil
- 2 tablespoons rice wine vinegar
- 1 teaspoon chili flakes (optional)

Instructions:
1. In a medium bowl, combine the soy sauce, brown sugar, garlic, ginger, sesame oil, rice wine vinegar, and chili flakes (if using).

2. Place the cubed beef short ribs in a large bowl and pour the teriyaki marinade over top. Mix everything together until the beef is well coated. Let the beef marinate for at least 30 minutes.
3. Preheat the grill to medium-high heat.
4. Thread the marinated beef cubes onto skewers. Grill the skewers for 5-7 minutes, or until the beef is cooked through and the outside is lightly charred.
5. Serve the teriyaki beef skewers hot with your favorite sides!

Nutrition Information:
Calories: 332 kcal, Carbohydrates: 11 g, Protein: 22 g, Fat: 19 g, Saturated Fat: 6 g, Cholesterol: 76 mg, Sodium: 2364 mg, Potassium: 511 mg, Fiber: 1 g, Sugar: 8 g, Vitamin C: 2 mg, Calcium: 28 mg, Iron: 3 mg

4. Greek-Style Beef Kabobs with Feta Cheese

Greek-Style Beef Kabobs with Feta Cheese is a flavorful, healthy, and hearty meal that will quickly become a family favorite. Not only bursting with flavor, this dish is also low in carb and loaded with protein and iron.
Serving: 4
Preparation Time: 15 minutes
Ready Time: 25 minutes

Ingredients:
-1 pound ground beef
-1/4 cup crumbled feta cheese
-1/4 cup finely chopped fresh parsley
-1/4 cup diced white onion
-2 cloves minced garlic
-1 teaspoon dried oregano
-1 teaspoon dried basil
-1/2 teaspoon salt
-1 tablespoon olive oil

Instructions:
1. Preheat your grill to medium-high heat.
2. In a large bowl, mix together the ground beef, feta cheese, parsley, onion, garlic, oregano, basil, salt, and olive oil until well combined.

3. Form the beef mixture into 4-6 patties, one inch thick.
4. Lightly oil grill grates and place kabob patties on the grill, cooking for 4-5 minutes per side, or until internal temperature reaches 160°F.
5. Remove patties from grill onto a plate, let rest for 5 minutes before serving.

Nutrition Information:
Calories: 301, Fat: 16g, Carbs: 3g, Protein: 28g, Fiber: 1g

5. Beef and Onion Kabobs

Beef and Onion Kabobs – juicy chunks of beef marinated in herbs and served with grilled onions. A delicious and easy dinner for any occasion!
Serving: 4
Preparation Time: 10 minutes
Ready Time: 30 minutes

Ingredients:
- 1 pound beef, cubed
- 1 onion, cut into large chunks
- 2 tablespoons olive oil
- 1 tablespoon balsamic vinegar
- 1/4 teaspoon garlic powder
- 1 teaspoon fresh parsley, chopped
- Salt and pepper

Instructions:
1. In a medium-sized bowl, combine beef, olive oil, balsamic vinegar, garlic powder, parsley, salt and pepper. Mix until evenly combined.
2. Preheat the grill to high heat.
3. Thread beef and onion onto separate skewers.
4. Place skewers on the grill and cook for 6 minutes per side or until beef is cooked to desired doneness.
5. Serve hot with your favorite accompaniments.

Nutrition Information:
Serving Size: 1/4 recipe
Calories: 310

Total Fat: 17.8g
Saturated Fat: 5.7g
Cholesterol: 92mg
Sodium: 167mg
Total Carbohydrates: 6.2g
Fiber: 0.7g
Sugar: 2.8g
Protein: 33.3g

6. Thai-Style Beef Satay Skewers

Thai-Style Beef Satay Skewers are an incredibly flavorful and easy-to-make dish, perfect for a summer BBQ or weeknight dinner. They take a classic Southeast Asian flavor combination and make it easy to enjoy right at home. This recipe yields 4 servings, takes 45 minutes in preparation, and cooks in 10 minutes.
Serving: 4
Preparation Time: 45 minutes
Ready Time: 10 minutes

Ingredients:
- 2 cloves garlic, minced
- 2 tablespoons freshly grated ginger root
- 2 tablespoons ground coriander
- 2 tablespoons ground cumin
- 2 tablespoons freshly chopped lemongrass
- 2 tablespoons brown sugar
- 2 tablespoons soy sauce
- 2 tablespoons vegetable oil
- 2 tablespoons freshly squeezed lime juice
- 1 lb. beef sirloin, cut into thin strips
- 8 wooden skewers, soaked in water for 30 minutes

Instructions:
1. In a large bowl, combine garlic, ginger, coriander, cumin, lemongrass, brown sugar, soy sauce, vegetable oil, and lime juice. Stir to create a marinade.
2. Place beef strips into the marinade and toss to coat evenly.

3. Cover and let marinate for 30 minutes up to 4 hours.
4. Heat a grill over medium-high heat.
5. Thread the beef strips onto the wooden skewers, ensuring that the pieces are securely held in place.
6. Grill for 5-7 minutes or until desired doneness is reached, flipping halfway through.
7. Serve hot, with extra lime wedges for squeezing.

Nutrition Information (per serving):
Calories: 370; Protein: 29.1g; Carbs: 15.1g; Fat: 21.9g; Saturated Fat: 5.8g; Sodium: 826mg; Potassium: 678mg; Fiber: 2.6g; Sugar: 6.2g; Vitamin A: 13IU; Vitamin C: 3.2mg; Calcium: 48mg; Iron: 3.2mg

7. Korean-Style Beef Bulgogi Skewers

Korean-Style Beef Bulgogi Skewers
Serving: 4
Preparation Time: 20 minutes
Ready Time: 10 minutes

Ingredients:
• 1 ½ pounds beef sirloin
• ½ cup soy sauce
• ¼ cup honey
• 2 tablespoons sesame oil
• 2 garlic cloves, minced
• 2 tablespoons freshly squeezed orange juice
• 2 teaspoons freshly grated ginger
• 1 teaspoon freshly ground pepper
• 2 green onions, finely chopped
• 12 wooden skewers

Instructions:
1. In a medium bowl, mix together soy sauce, honey, sesame oil, garlic, orange juice, ginger, pepper, and green onions.
2. Cut the beef sirloin into 2-inch cubes and place them in a shallow dish or bowl.

3. Pour the marinade over the beef cubes and mix together until the beef is evenly coated.
4. Cover the dish with plastic wrap and let marinade in the refrigerator for at least 30 minutes, or up to 8 hours for more flavor.
5. Soak 12 wooden skewers in water for at least 10 minutes.
6. Preheat a grill to high heat.
7. Thread the beef cubes on the skewers and grill, turning frequently, until desired doneness is reached, about 8 minutes.

Nutrition Information:
• Calories: 360 kcal
• Protein: 34 g
• Fat: 16 g
• Carbohydrates: 16 g

8. Beef and Bell Pepper Skewers

These flavorful amazing Beef and Bell Pepper Skewers make the perfect meal or appetizer for any occasion. Marinated beef cubes are paired with bell peppers and skewered together and then grilled to perfection.
Serving: Makes 4 skewers
Preparation Time: 10 minutes
Ready Time: 20 minutes

Ingredients:
– 1 lb. beef cubes
– 2 bell peppers, cut into 1-inch cubes
– 2 garlic cloves, minced
– 4 tbsp. soy sauce
– 2 tbsp. olive oil
– 2 tbsp. balsamic vinegar
– 2 tsp. fresh parsley, finely minced
– 1 tsp. ground black pepper

Instructions:
1. In a large bowl, combine beef cubes, bell peppers, garlic, soy sauce, olive oil, balsamic vinegar, parsley and ground black pepper. Toss to combine and coat the Ingredients completely.

2. Preheat grill to medium-high heat. Thread the beef and bell pepper cubes onto 4 skewers, alternating between the two Ingredients. Place skewers on the preheated grill and cook for about 8-10 minutes or until the beef cubes are cooked through and the bell peppers are lightly charred.
3. Serve skewers with desired side dishes and enjoy!

Nutrition Information:
Calories: 310, Fat: 18 g, Carbohydrates: 8 g, Protein: 27 g, Sodium: 1592 mg

9. Mediterranean Beef Kabobs with Olives and Feta Cheese

These Mediterranean Beef Kabobs feature delicious cubes of beef, kalamata olives, dried oregano, tomatoes and feta, grilled to perfection and served over a bed of saffron rice.

Serving: 4
Preparation Time: 10 minutes
Ready Time: 25 minutes

Ingredients:
- 1 pound of sirloin, cubed
- 1 tablespoon of olive oil
- 1 teaspoon of garlic, finely chopped
- 1 teaspoon of oregano
- 1/2 teaspoon of salt
- 1/2 teaspoon of pepper
- 8 kalamata olives, pitted
- 4 Roma tomatoes, quartered
- 2 tablespoons of crumbled feta

Instructions:
1. Preheat your outdoor grill or an indoor griddle over medium heat.
2. Place the cubed sirloin in a bowl. Add the olive oil, garlic, oregano, salt, and pepper. Toss until the steak is evenly coated.

3. Thread the beef cubes, olives, tomatoes and feta onto 4 metal or wooden skewers.
4. Place the skewers onto the hot grill and cook for 8-10 minutes, flipping once during cooking.
5. Serve warm over a bed of saffron rice. Enjoy!

Nutrition Information: Per Serving: Calories: 315, Protein: 24g, Total Fat: 16g, Sat. Fat: 5g, Sodium: 472mg, Carbohydrates: 8g, Fiber: 2g, Sugar: 3g

10. Beef and Zucchini Skewers

Beef and Zucchini Skewers
Serving: 6
Preparation Time: 10 minutes
Ready Time: 20 minutes

Ingredients:
- 1lb beef sirloin or flank steak, cut into 8 cubes
- 2 zucchinis, cut into 8 cubes
- 2 tbsp olive oil
- 1 tsp garlic powder
- 1 tsp Italian seasoning
- ¼ tsp sea salt
- ¼ tsp black pepper

Instructions:
1. Preheat a charcoal or gas grill to medium-high heat.
2. In a large bowl, mix together the beef cubes, zucchini cubes, olive oil, garlic powder, Italian seasoning, sea salt, and black pepper.
3. Skewer the beef and zucchini cubes onto 6 metal skewers.
4. Place the skewers on the grill and cook for about 10 minutes, turning occasionally until the beef is cooked through and the zucchini is lightly charred.
5. Serve hot with your favorite side dishes.

Nutrition Information:

Calories: 189kcal, Carbohydrates: 3g, Protein: 23g, Fat: 9g, Saturated Fat: 2g, Cholesterol: 62mg, Sodium: 198mg, Potassium: 463mg, Fiber: 1g, Sugar: 2g, Vitamin A: 133IU, Vitamin C: 16mg, Calcium: 25mg, Iron: 2mg.

11. Jamaican Jerk Beef Skewers

Get ready – it's time to bring the flavors of the Caribbean to your kitchen with these delicious Jamaican Jerk Beef Skewers. The bold spices combined with the smoky Caribbean-inspired jerk sauce are sure to make any meal irresistible!
Serving: 4 Servings
Preparation Time: 45 minutes
Ready Time: 2 hours

Ingredients:
• 2 lbs of beef sirloin, cubed
• 1/2 cup of jerk marinade
• 1 tablespoon of olive oil
• 2 tablespoons of lime juice
• 1 teaspoon of garlic powder
• 1 teaspoon of onion powder
• 2 tablespoons of brown sugar
• 1 teaspoon of chili powder
• 2 tablespoons of freshly chopped cilantro
• 4 skewers

Instructions:
1. In a medium bowl, mix together all of the Ingredients until everything is evenly coated.
2. Let the meat marinate for at least 2 hours in the fridge.
3. Thread the beef onto the skewers, making sure to keep the cubes close together.
4. Heat up a grill pan to medium high heat and brush with olive oil.
5. Grill the skewers for about 5-7 minutes on each side, or until the beef is cooked to your liking.
6. Serve the skewers and enjoy!

Nutrition Information:
• Calories: 327kcal
• Carbohydrates: 10g
• Protein: 28g
• Fat: 17g
• Saturated Fat: 6g
• Trans Fat: 0g
• Cholesterol: 85mg
• Sodium: 465mg
• Potassium: 484mg
• Fiber: 1g
• Sugar: 6g
• Vitamin A: 311IU
• Vitamin C: 7mg
• Calcium: 25mg
• Iron: 2mg

12. Beef and Potato Skewers

Beef and Potato Skewers is a hearty meal that is quick and easy to prepare. It's the perfect dish to put on the grill this summer for a delicious meal.

Serving: 4
Preparation time: 10 minutes
Ready time: 20 minutes

Ingredients:
- 500g diced beef
- 500g diced potatoes
- 2 tbsp olive oil
- 1 clove of garlic, minced
- 2 tsp smoked paprika
- 2 tsp cumin
- Salt and pepper to taste

Instructions:
1. Preheat your grill to medium-high heat.

2. In a bowl, stir together the beef, potatoes, olive oil, garlic, smoked paprika, cumin, salt, and pepper.
3. Thread the beef and potatoes onto metal skewers.
4. Place the skewers on the grill and cook for 8-10 minutes, turning occasionally, until the beef is cooked through and the potatoes are lightly charred and tender.
5. Serve the skewers hot and enjoy!

Nutrition Information:
(Per 1 Skewer): Calories: 140, Total Fat: 5g, Cholesterol: 25mg, Sodium: 60mg, Total Carbohydrate: 9g, Protein 14g.

13. Chimichurri Beef Skewers

Chimichurri Beef Skewers
Serving: 4
Preparation Time: 10 minutes
Ready Time: 10 minutes

Ingredients:
- 1-1/2 pounds boneless beef sirloin
- 1/2 cup chimichurri sauce
- 1 teaspoon smoked paprika
- 1 large red bell pepper, cubed
- 2 tablespoons olive oil
- 1 teaspoon each ground cumin and black pepper
- 2 cloves garlic, minced
- Salt to taste

Instructions:
1. Preheat grill to medium high heat.
2. Cut beef into 1-inch cubes. Place beef cubes in a bowl and season with smoked paprika, cumin, pepper, garlic, and salt. Mix together until evenly coated.
3. Thread beef cubes onto skewers.
4. Brush skewers with olive oil and place on the preheated grill. Grill for about 6 minutes or until desired doneness is reached, flipping once.

5. Place bell pepper cubes on the grill and cook for about 3 minutes or until tender.
6. Drizzle beef skewers with chimichurri sauce and serve immediately with the bell pepper cubes.

Nutrition Information (per serving):
Calories: 418; Total Fat: 24g; Saturated Fat: 7g; Cholesterol: 98mg; Sodium: 368mg; Carbohydrates: 6g; Fiber: 1g; Sugar: 1g; Protein: 34g

14. Beef and Pineapple Skewers

This delicious recipe for Beef and Pineapple Skewers is a great addition to any cookout or dinner party. It's always a hit with adults and kids alike.
Serving: 5
Preparation Time: 10 minutes
Ready Time: 25 minutes

Ingredients:
• 500g beef sirloin, cut into cubes
• 2 pineapples, cubed
• 1 teaspoon garlic powder
• 1 tablespoon coconut oil
• 5 wooden skewers
• Salt and pepper, to taste

Instructions:
1. Preheat the grill to a medium-high heat and grease it.
2. In a medium bowl, mix together the beef cubes, pineapple cubes, garlic powder, coconut oil, salt and pepper until all the Ingredients are evenly distributed.
3. Divide the mixture onto each of the skewer and carefully thread it onto the skewer.
4. Place the skewers onto the preheated grill and cook for 10-15 minutes, turning occasionally, until the beef is cooked through.
5. Serve warm and enjoy.

Nutrition Information: 326 calories, 22g protein, 22g carbohydrates, 17g fat

15. Indian-Style Beef Seekh Kabobs

Indian-Style Beef Seekh Kabobs are succulent and juicy kebabs made with a flavorful and aromatic blend of spices and minced beef. This classic, beloved dish is sure to please any palate.
Serving: 4-6 servings
Preparation Time: 15 minutes
Ready Time: 35 minutes

Ingredients:
- 1 lb ground beef
- 2 cloves garlic, minced
- 2 tsp freshly grated ginger
- 1 tsp garam masala
- 1 tsp ground cumin
- 1 tsp ground coriander
- 1/2 tsp ground turmeric
- 1/2 tsp ground cardamom
- 1/2 tsp chili powder
- 1/2 tsp ground black pepper
- 1/2 tsp salt
- 1 small onion, finely chopped
- 2 Tbsp vegetable oil

Instructions:
1. In a bowl, combine the minced beef, garlic, ginger, garam masala, cumin, coriander, turmeric, cardamom, chili powder, black pepper, and salt.
2. Add the chopped onion to the mixture. Mix until all the Ingredients are evenly distributed.
3. Divide the mixture into 8 equal portions.
4. Grease your hands with some vegetable oil. Using a greased surface, shape each portion of the mixture into a cylindrical kabob shape (like a sausage).

5. Heat a skillet over medium-high heat. Add the vegetable oil and let it warm up.
6. Add the kabobs to the skillet and cook for 8-10 minutes, flipping them at regular intervals.
7. Cook until the kabobs are cooked through and nicely browned.

Nutrition Information: Servings: 4-6, Amount per Serving: Calories: 106, Total fat: 5.9, Saturated fat: 2g, Cholesterol: 18mg, Sodium: 198mg, Total carbohydrate: 4.4g, Dietary fiber: 0.8g, Sugars: 0.5g, Protein: 8.2g

16. Beef and Cherry Tomato Skewers

Make this easy and delicious Beef and Cherry Tomato Skewers dish for your next dinner night. This skewered specialty is ready to be served with a creamy dip in just about 30 minutes!
Serving: 4 skewers
Preparation Time: 10 minutes
Ready Time: 30 minutes

Ingredients:
-1/4 cup extra-virgin olive oil
-2 tablespoons lemon juice
-1 teaspoon Italian seasoning
-1/2 teaspoon minced garlic
-1/4 teaspoon salt
-1/4 teaspoon ground black pepper
-1 pound beef sirloin steak, cut into 4 cubes
-20 cherry tomatoes

Instructions:
1. In a medium bowl, whisk together olive oil, lemon juice, Italian seasoning, garlic, salt and black pepper to make a marinade.
2. Place beef cubes in the bowl, cover and let marinade for 20 minutes.
3. Preheat BBQ or grill.
4. Place beef cubes and cherry tomatoes on separate skewers.
5. Spray Skewers with cooking oil.
6. Grill on each side for 5 minutes or until cooked through.

Nutrition Information:
Calories: 316, Total Fat: 18.4 g, Saturated Fat: 4 g, Cholesterol: 74 mg, Sodium: 201 mg, Total Carbohydrate: 7.7 g, Dietary Fiber: 1 g, Sugars: 3.7 g, Protein: 26.2 g.

17. Beef and Eggplant Kabobs

Beef and Eggplant Kabobs are a delicious and easy to make kabob recipe. With a combination of savory beef, eggplant and sweet peppers, this dish is sure to please even the pickiest eaters.
Serving: 4
Preparation Time: 10 minutes
Ready Time: 40 minutes

Ingredients:
- 1 lb of boneless beef sirloin or chuck, cut into 1-inch cubes
- 1 large eggplant, cut into 1-inch cubes
- 2 green bell peppers, cut into 1-inch cubes
- 2 cloves of garlic, minced
- 1 teaspoon of ground cumin
- 1 teaspoon of dried oregano
- 1 tablespoon of olive oil
- Salt and pepper, to taste

Instructions:
1. Preheat the oven to 375°F.
2. On a large sheet pan, combine all of the Ingredients and toss to mix.
3. Place the kabobs onto a greased roasting pan.
4. Bake the kabobs for about 35-40 minutes, or until the beef is cooked through and the vegetables are tender.
5. Serve the kabobs with your favorite sides and enjoy!

Nutrition Information:
Calories Per Serving: 225, Total Fat: 8.3 g, Saturated Fat: 2.7 g, Cholesterol: 43 mg, Sodium: 1.3 mg, Total Carbohydrates: 13.2 g, Dietary Fiber: 4.6 g, Protein: 22.9 g

18. Hoisin Glazed Beef Skewers

Hoisin Glazed Beef Skewers is an easy to make and flavorful dish made with marinated beef pierced on skewers and cooked in a homemade spicy hoisin glaze. This dish is best served with cooked white rice and vegetables.

Serving: 4
Preparation Time: 25 minutes
Ready Time: 10 minutes

Ingredients:
- 1 lb flank steak, sliced into thin strips
- 2 tablespoons hoisin sauce
- 2 tablespoons honey
- 2 tablespoons soy sauce
- 1 teaspoon garlic, minced
- 1 teaspoon fresh ginger, minced
- 1 tablespoon sesame oil
- 2 tablespoons vegetable oil
- 4 wooden skewers

Instructions:
1. Start by placing the steak strips into a bowl and combine the hoisin sauce, honey, soy sauce, garlic, ginger, sesame oil, and vegetable oil in a separate bowl.
2. Pour the marinade over the steak strips and stir to coat.
3. Let the steak strips marinate for at least 30 minutes or up to 4 hours,the longer you marinate the richer the flavor.
4. Preheat an outdoor grill to high heat.
5. Thread the steak strips onto the skewers.
6. Grill the steak skewers for 4-5 minutes per side, or until cooked through.
7. Drizzle the remaining marinade over the steak skewers and continue grilling for another couple of minutes.
8. Serve the steak skewers with cooked white rice and vegetables.

Nutrition Information:
Calories: 406

Protein: 30g
Fat: 19g
Carbohydrate: 22g

19. Beef and Carrot Skewers

Beef and Carrot Skewers
This delicious meal of lightly seasoned beef skewers with chunks of juicy carrots are as flavor-packed as they are colorful! A mouthwatering dish that your family will love, these beef and carrot skewers are quick and easy to make.
Serving: 4
Preparation Time: 10 minutes
Ready Time: 25 minutes

Ingredients:
- 1 pounds beef sirloin steaks, cut into 2-inch cubes
- 2 tablespoons olive oil
- 1 teaspoon garlic powder
- 1 teaspoon paprika
- 1 teaspoon salt
- 1/2 teaspoon ground black pepper
- 2 large carrots, cut into 2-inch chunks
- 4 wooden skewers

Instructions:
1. Preheat oven to 400°F.
2. In a medium bowl, mix together the olive oil, garlic powder, paprika, salt, and pepper. Add the beef cubes and carrots and toss until Ingredients are well coated.
3. Thread the beef cubes and carrots onto the skewers.
4. Place the skewers on a baking sheet and bake for 25 minutes, flipping the skewers halfway through.

Nutrition Information (per serving):
Calories: 250
Fat: 14g
Carbohydrates: 8g

Protein: 22g
Sodium: 640mg
Fiber: 2g

20. Soy-Glazed Beef Kabobs with Sesame Seeds

Soy-Glazed Beef Kabobs with Sesame Seeds is a delicious main course dish with a tantalizing soy and garlic marinade and a fragrant sprinkle of sesame seeds. It's perfect for dinner parties or a summer BBQ.
Serving: 4
Preparation Time: 10 minutes
Ready Time: 1 hour

Ingredients:
- 4 sirloin steaks, cut into bite-sized cubes
- 2 garlic cloves, minced
- 2 tablespoons olive oil
- 2 tablespoons low-sodium soy sauce
- 2 tablespoons dark brown sugar
- 2 tablespoons freshly squeezed lime juice
- 1 teaspoon chili powder
- 1 teaspoon ground ginger
- 2 tablespoons toasted sesame seeds

Instructions:
1. In a medium bowl, combine the garlic, olive oil, soy sauce, brown sugar, lime juice, chili powder, and ginger. Mix well.
2. Place the steak cubes into a shallow dish or a large resealable bag. Pour the marinade over the steak cubes and mix until the beef is fully coated. Marinate for 30-60 minutes in the refrigerator.
3. Preheat the grill to medium-high heat. Grease the grate with oil.
4. Place the steak cubes onto skewers and place on the preheated grill. Cook for 4-7 minutes, flipping once to ensure even cooking.
5. Sprinkle the sesame seeds over the steak kabobs and cook for an additional minute or until the desired doneness is achieved.

Nutrition Information:

Amount Per Serving: 343 calories; 16.5g fat; 11.9g carbohydrates; 29.7g protein; 3.8mg cholesterol; 518mg sodium.

21. Beef and Broccoli Skewers

These Beef and Broccoli Skewers are the perfect combination of tender beef and crunchy broccoli, all threaded onto skewers and roasted until tender and juicy.
Serving: 4-6 servings
Preparation Time: 10 minutes
Ready Time: 25 minutes

Ingredients:
- 2 large bell peppers, any color
- 1 1/2 lbs beef (sirloin, flank, or other cut), cut into 1-inch cubes
- 2 heads broccoli, cut into florets
- 1/4 cup olive oil
- 1/4 cup balsamic vinegar
- 2 tsp dried Italian herbs
- 2 cloves garlic, finely minced
- 1/4 tsp salt
- 1/4 tsp black pepper

Instructions:
1. Preheat oven to 400F.
2. In a large bowl combine the bell peppers, beef cubes, broccoli, olive oil, balsamic vinegar, Italian herbs, garlic, salt and pepper. Mix together until everything is combined.
3. Thread the beef and vegetables onto skewers, alternating between beef cubes and vegetables.
4. Place skewers on a baking tray lined with parchment paper and bake for 20-25 minutes, or until beef is cooked through and vegetables are lightly browned.

Nutrition Information (per serving):
Calories 286, Fat 16g, Carbohydrate 9g, Protein 25g, Sodium 131mg

22. Balsamic Glazed Beef and Mushroom Skewers

Balsamic Glazed Beef and Mushroom Skewers are savory and juicy kabobs that make for a great weeknight dinner or a meal to be enjoyed outside at a backyard barbecue.
Serving: Makes 8 skewers
Preparation Time: 10 minutes
Ready Time: 40 minutes

Ingredients:
- 1/2 cup balsamic vinegar
- 3 tablespoons olive oil
- 2 tablespoons brown sugar
- 3 cloves garlic, minced
- 2 teaspoons fresh thyme or 1 teaspoon dried thyme
- 1 teaspoon smoked paprika
- Salt and freshly ground black pepper, to taste
- 1 pound sirloin steak, cut into 1-inch cubes
- 8 ounces cremini mushrooms, stems removed
- 8 metal or bamboo skewers

Instructions:
1. In a large bowl, whisk together balsamic vinegar, olive oil, brown sugar, garlic, thyme, paprika, salt, and pepper.
2. Add the steak cubes and stir to combine. Cover the bowl and refrigerate 1-2 hours.
3. Preheat grill over medium-high heat.
4. Thread steak and mushrooms onto skewers and brush with marinade.
5. Grill for 10 minutes, flipping skewers once.
6. Drizzle with extra balsamic glaze and serve!

Nutrition Information:
Per Serving: Calories 202, Total Fat 11g, Total Carbohydrate 11g, Protein 14g, Cholesterol 39mg, Sodium 88mg.

23. Beef and Asparagus Skewers

Beef and Asparagus Skewers – tasty skewers of beef and asparagus sure to be a hit with the family! Perfect for grilling or roasting, these skewers are easy to make and the tender beef and crisp asparagus make a delicious combination.

Serving: 4

Preparation Time: 15 minutes

Ready Time: 30 minutes

Ingredients:

-500g beef, cubed

-400g asparagus, trimmed

-2 cloves garlic, minced

-1 onion, diced

-3 tbsp vegetable oil

-2 tbsp soy sauce

-1 tsp fresh ground black pepper

-2 tsp fresh thyme

Instructions:

1. Preheat oven to 200°C (400°F).

2. Combine beef cubes, asparagus, garlic, onion, and oil in a large bowl. Mix until Ingredients are fully combined.

3. Season with soy sauce and black pepper.

4. Alternately thread beef cubes and asparagus onto wooden skewers.

5. Place skewers on a baking sheet and sprinkle with fresh thyme.

6. Bake in preheated oven for 25-30 minutes, or until beef is cooked through.

7. Serve hot and enjoy!

Nutrition Information:

Calories: 200; Total Fat: 10g; Saturated Fat: 2g; Cholesterol: 40mg; Sodium: 360mg; Carbohydrates: 4g; Fiber: 2g; Protein: 20g

24. Red Wine Marinated Beef Kabobs

Red Wine Marinated Beef Kabobs are a delicious and easy way to enjoy steak on the grill. Marinating the beef in red wine and herbs adds flavor and tenderizes the meat for the perfect kabob. This recipe serves 4

people and takes about 15 minutes to prepare, with an additional 30 minutes of marinating time, with ready time of 45 minutes.
Serving: 4
Preparation Time: 15 minutes
Ready Time: 45 minutes

Ingredients:
- 1 1/2 pounds of sirloin steak, cut into 1 inch cubes
- 1/3 cup red wine
- 2 tablespoons Worcestershire sauce
- 2 cloves garlic, minced
- 1 teaspoon dried oregano
- 1 teaspoon dried thyme
- 1 teaspoon dried rosemary
- 1/2 teaspoon ground black pepper
- 1 tablespoon olive oil
- 4 wooden skewers soaked in water for 30 minutes

Instructions:
1. In a medium bowl, whisk together the red wine, Worcestershire sauce, garlic, oregano, thyme, rosemary, pepper and olive oil.
2. Add the cubes of steak to the marinade and mix until the steak cubes have been fully coated. Cover and allow the steak to marinate for at least 30 minutes.
3. Preheat the grill to medium-high heat.
4. Thread each of the soaked skewers with steak cubes, leaving some space between each cube.
5. Grill the kabobs for about 4 minutes per side, or until the steak cubes are cooked to your desired doneness.
6. Serve warm.

Nutrition Information: Per serving, these Red Wine Marinated Beef Kabobs contain 291 calories, 18.4g of fat, 3.8g of carbohydrates, 21.0g of protein, and 62.7mg of sodium.

25. Beef and Summer Squash Skewers

Beef and Summer Squash Skewers: There is no better way to enjoy the summer than with a delicious grilled dish of beef and summer squash skewers. The savory marinade of garlic and fresh herbs, tender chunks of beef, and grilled summer squash on juicy skewers is always a hit! This dish serves four.

Serving: 4

Preparation Time: 15 minutes

Ready Time: 30 minutes

Ingredients:
- 1/4 cup olive oil
- 2 cloves garlic, minced
- 1 teaspoon Italian seasoning
- Salt and pepper, to taste
- 1 1/2 lbs. beef sirloin, cut into cubes
- 2 medium summer squash, cut into cubes
- 8 bamboo skewers

Instructions:
1. In a medium bowl, whisk together the olive oil, garlic, Italian seasoning, salt, and pepper.
2. Place beef cubes into the bowl and toss to coat in the marinade. Cover the bowl with plastic wrap and store in the refrigerator for 15 minutes.
3. Set your grill to low-medium heat.
4. In a separate bowl, toss the summer squash cubes in the remaining marinade.
5. Thread beef cubes and summer squash cubes onto bamboo skewers.
6. Place the skewers onto an oiled grill and cook, flipping once, until both beef cubes and summer squash cubes are cooked through and lightly browned, about 7-8 minutes.
7. Serve hot with your favorite dipping sauce.

Nutrition Information:
Calories: 295, Total Fat: 19g, Saturated Fat: 6g, Cholesterol: 79mg, Sodium: 157mg, Potassium: 10mg, Carbohydrates: 8g, Fiber: 2g, Sugar: 3g, Protein: 24g, Vitamin A: 13%, Vitamin C: 16%, Calcium: 2%, Iron: 18%

26. Moroccan Spiced Beef Skewers

Spruce up a traditional kebab with this Moroccan spiced version!
Featuring the fragrant flavors of cumin, coriander, turmeric and harissa,
these beef skewers are perfect for a summertime barbecue.
Serving: 4 people
Preparation Time: 10 minutes
Ready Time: 2 hours

Ingredients:
•2 lbs beef sirloin, cut into 1-inch cubes
•3 tablespoons cumin
•2 tablespoons coriander
•1 teaspoon turmeric
•2 tablespoons olive oil
•1/2 teaspoon Maldon salt
•1/4 cup harissa paste

Instructions:
1. In a large bowl, combine the beef cubes, cumin, coriander, turmeric,
olive oil, salt and harissa paste until evenly coated.
2. Place the beef cubes onto metal or bamboo skewers, then place onto a
platter and chill in the refrigerator for at least 2 hours.
3. Heat up a barbecue or grill to a medium heat.
4. Place the beef skewers onto the grill and cook for about 4 minutes, or
until cooked to your liking.
5. Serve with a dollop of harissa and a sprinkle of sea salt.

**Nutrition Information: per serving: Calories: 370, Protein: 36g, Fat:
17g, Carbs: 8g, Fiber: 2g, Sugar: 2g, Sodium: 490mg**

27. Beef and Artichoke Heart Kabobs

Get your summer grilling season started early with these easy yet
delicious Beef and Artichoke Heart Kabobs.
Serving: 4
Preparation time: 10 minutes
Ready time: 20 minutes

Ingredients:
- 1 pound flank steak, cut into 1-inch cubes
- 2 cups fresh artichoke hearts
- 2 bell peppers, cut into 1-inch cubes
- 2 tablespoons olive oil
- 2 tablespoons chopped fresh herbs such as rosemary, thyme, oregano, or sage
- 2 cloves garlic, minced
- Salt and pepper, to taste

Instructions:
1. Preheat the grill to medium-high heat.
2. Place the cubes of flank steak, artichoke hearts, and bell peppers in a large bowl.
3. Drizzle with olive oil and sprinkle with herbs and garlic. Toss to coat and season with salt and pepper.
4. Thread the beef and vegetables onto metal skewers, alternating between steak and vegetables.
5. Place the skewers on the grill and cook for 10-12 minutes, flipping once during cooking.
6. Serve hot with your favorite sides.

Nutrition Information:
Calories: 254
Fat: 13g
Carbohydrates: 8g
Protein: 24g
Sodium: 411mg

28. Rosemary Garlic Beef Skewers

Rosemary Garlic Beef Skewers
This delicious beef and vegetable combination infused with rosemary and garlic will tantalize your taste buds and have your friends and family begging for more. Serve with your favorite stir fry or over rice for a quick and easy meal.
Serving: 4

Preparation Time: 15 mins
Ready Time: 30 mins

Ingredients:
-1 lb. beef sirloin steak
-1/4 cup extra-virgin olive oil
-2 tablespoons fresh rosemary, finely chopped
-2 cloves garlic, minced
-1 teaspoon freshly-ground black pepper
-1/2 teaspoon sea salt
-2 bell peppers (any color), cut into 1-inch chunks
-1 large onion, cut into 1-inch chunks
- metal or wooden skewers

Instructions:
1. Preheat grill to medium high heat.
2. Cut beef into 1-inch cubes and place in large bowl.
3. In a small bowl, whisk together olive oil, rosemary, garlic, pepper, and salt. Pour over beef cubes and mix to combine.
4. Assemble the skewers by alternating pieces of beef and vegetables.
5. Grill skewers over medium-high heat for 10-12 minutes, flipping once halfway through to ensure even cooking.
6. Serve hot with your favorite vegetables or sides, and enjoy!

Nutrition Information:
Per Serving: Calories 350, Total Fat 19g (Saturated 4g, Trans 0g), Cholesterol 77mg, Sodium 364mg, Total Carbs 14g, Dietary Fiber 4g, Protein 27g, Vitamin A 36%, Vitamin C 147%, Calcium 6%, Iron 16%

29. Beef and Green Bean Skewers

Beef and Green Bean Skewers
Serving: 4
Preparation Time: 10 minutes
Ready Time: 25 minutes

Ingredients:
• 500g beef steak, sliced

- 1 garlic clove, crushed
- ½ teaspoon of cumin
- 2 tablespoons olive oil
- 1 teaspoon paprika
- 2 teaspoon ground coriander
- 300g green beans
- 2 tablespoons soy sauce
- 2 tablespoons honey

Instructions:
1. In a bowl, combine the garlic, cumin, olive oil, paprika and ground coriander.
2. Add the steak slices to the bowl and turn them in the spice mixture, so they're well coated.
3. Slice the beans into 2-3cm pieces.
4. Preheat the oven to 200C.
5. Thread the beef and beans alternately onto wooden skewers.
6. Place the skewers onto a baking tray and season with the soy sauce and honey.
7. Roast for 20 minutes, turning them halfway through.

Nutrition Information:
Calories: 293 kcal | Carbohydrates: 23.3 g | Protein: 29.6 g | Fat: 8.9 g | Cholesterol: 55 mg | Sodium: 568 mg | Potassium: 569 mg | Fiber: 4.1 g | Sugar: 9.9 g

30. BBQ Beef Kabobs with Bacon

Try something new with your weekly BBQ night with our delicious BBQ beef kabobs with bacon! These kabobs are sure to please the whole family with the perfect combination of beef, bacon, and flavorful BBQ sauce.
Serving: 4
Preparation Time: 25 minutes
Ready Time: 45 minutes

Ingredients:
- 1 (16-ounce) package pre-cooked bacon

- 2 pounds beef sirloin steak, cut into 1-inch cubes
- 2 bell peppers, cut into 1-inch pieces
- 2 large onions, cut into 1-inch pieces
- 1/4 cup barbecue sauce
- 2 tablespoons oil
- 1/2 tablespoon garlic powder
- 2 tablespoons brown sugar
- Salt and pepper to taste

Instructions:
1. Preheat oven to 375° F.
2. Place bacon in a single layer on a parchment-lined baking sheet.
3. Bake for 25 minutes, until crispy.
4. In a large bowl, combine beef cubes, bell peppers, onions, barbecue sauce, oil, garlic powder, and brown sugar. Season with salt and pepper, to taste.
5. Thread beef cubes, bacon, peppers, and onions onto metal or wooden skewers, alternating Ingredients.
6. Preheat grill to medium-high heat.
7. Grill kabobs 10-15 minutes, flipping occasionally, until beef is cooked through.

Nutrition Information: per serving: Calories: 380, Total Fat: 17g, Saturated Fat: 5g, Sodium: 621mg, Carbohydrates: 10g, Protein: 43g, Cholesterol: 79mg, Fiber: 2g.

31. Beef and Cauliflower Skewers

Enjoy this tasty yet healthy Beef and Cauliflower Skewers dish with a mixture of flavors and textures. A fantastic dinner for any night of the week!
Serving: 4-6
Preparation Time: 10 minutes
Ready Time: 25 minutes

Ingredients:
• 1 lb ground beef
• 1 large head of cauliflower, broken into florets

- 2 tablespoons olive oil
- Salt and pepper, to taste
- 1 teaspoon garlic powder
- 1 teaspoon onion powder
- 1 teaspoon smoked paprika
- 1 teaspoon dried oregano

Instructions:
1. Preheat the oven to 375 degrees F.
2. In a large bowl, mix together the ground beef, salt, pepper, garlic powder, onion powder, smoked paprika, and oregano.
3. Grab a handful of the beef mixture and form it into a patty shape before wrapping it around a piece of cauliflower floret.
4. Repeat until all of the cauliflower florets have been wrapped with the beef mixture.
5. Place the skewers on a greased baking sheet and brush with the olive oil.
6. Bake for 25 minutes, flipping halfway through the baking time, until the beef is cooked through.

Nutrition Information:
Calories: 250; Total Fat: 14 g; Cholesterol: 70 mg; Sodium: 130 mg; Total Carbohydrates: 8 g; Protein: 22 g.

32. Honey Mustard Beef Kabobs

Honey Mustard Beef Kabobs - Take your grilled meat to the next level with this easy and flavorful kabob recipe! Simple to prepare and ready for dinner in under 30 minutes, these kabobs will be a crowd pleaser.
Serving: 8
Preparation time: 15 minutes
Ready time: 30 minutes

Ingredients:
- 1 lb. lean beef steak, cubed
- 2 tablespoons olive oil
- ⅓ cup honey mustard
- 2 cloves garlic, minced

- 2 tablespoons fresh parsley, minced
- 1 teaspoon Italian seasoning
- ½ teaspoon sea salt
- ½ teaspoon black pepper

Instructions:
1. Preheat your grill to medium heat.
2. In a large bowl, combine the cubed steak, olive oil, honey mustard, garlic, parsley, Italian seasoning, sea salt, and black pepper.
3. Allow to marinate for 10 minutes while you assemble skewers.
4. Thread the cubed steak onto metal skewers.
5. Place kabobs on the grill and cook for 7 minutes per side or until they reach desired doneness.
6. Serve and enjoy!

Nutrition Information:
- Calories: 147 kcal
- Carbohydrates: 5.4 g
- Protein: 15.1 g
- Fat: 6.7 g
- Sodium: 210 mg
- Potassium: 178 mg

33. Beef and Sweet Potato Skewers

Beef and Sweet Potato Skewers
Serving: 4
Preparation Time: 10 minutes
Ready Time: 30 minutes

Ingredients:
- 1 lb. ground beef
- 1 sweet potato, peeled and cubed into small cubes
- ¼ cup olive oil
- 1 teaspoon smoked paprika
- 1 teaspoon onion powder
- ½ teaspoon garlic powder
- ½ teaspoon ground cumin

- ½ teaspoon ground coriander
- Salt and pepper, to taste

Instructions:
1. Preheat oven to 375°F.
2. In a large bowl, mix together ground beef, sweet potato cubes, olive oil, paprika, onion powder, garlic powder, cumin, coriander, salt, and pepper until fully combined.
3. Divide the mixture into four parts and form into kebabs on wooden skewers.
4. Bake in preheated oven for 25-30 minutes, or until ground beef is cooked through and sweet potatoes are soft and browned.
5. Serve.

Nutrition Information:
Calories: 370
Fat: 19 g
Carbohydrates: 18 g
Protein: 27 g

34. Cuban-Style Beef Skewers with Mojo Sauce

Cuban-Style Beef Skewers with Mojo Sauce is a traditional Caribbean dish that is packed full of flavor. Perfect for summer grilling or a party, these juicy beef skewers are sure to please the taste buds.
Serving: 8
Preparation Time: 20 minutes
Ready Time: 45 minutes

Ingredients:
- 2 pounds sirloin steak, cut into 1-inch cubes
- 1/2 cup olive oil
- 2 tablespoons ground cumin
- 2 teaspoons ground coriander
- 2 teaspoons smoked paprika
- 1 teaspoon garlic powder
- 1/2 teaspoon dried oregano
- 1/2 cup freshly squeezed orange juice

- Zest of 1 orange
- 2 tablespoons white vinegar
- 1/4 cup freshly chopped cilantro leaves
- Juice of one lime
- Salt to taste

Instructions:
1. In a large bowl, combine the olive oil, cumin, coriander, smoked paprika, garlic powder, oregano, orange juice, orange zest and vinegar. Stir until fully combined.
2. Place the cubed steak into the bowl and stir to coat all the pieces evenly.
3. Thread the steak cubes onto metal or wooden skewers.
4. Heat a grill or grill pan to medium-high heat, and fry the skewers for 4-5 minutes per side, or until the steak has reached the desired doneness.
5. Meanwhile, in a small bowl, combine the cilantro, lime juice and salt.
6. Once the skewers are cooked, brush the mojo sauce over the skewers and serve them hot.

Nutrition Information (per serving):
Calories: 295; Protein: 28g; Fat: 11.4g; Carbs: 9.7g; Sodium: 108mg

35. Beef and Cabbage Skewers

Beef and Cabbage Skewers
These flavorful Beef and Cabbage Skewers are packed with flavor from savory beef, crunchy cabbage and a tangy teriyaki glaze. They're simple enough for a quick weeknight dinner, but also make an impressive appetizer or main course at any gathering.
Serving: 6
Preparation Time: 10 minutes
Ready Time: 15-20 minutes

Ingredients:
- 1/4 cup soy sauce
- 2 tablespoons honey
- 2 tablespoons teriyaki sauce
- 1 clove garlic, minced

- 1/4 teaspoon ground ginger
- 1 pound lean ground beef
- 2 cups thinly sliced cabbage
- 2 green onions, finely sliced
- 6-8 bamboo skewers

Instructions:
1. Preheat the broiler for high heat.
2. In a small bowl, whisk together the soy sauce, honey, teriyaki sauce, garlic and ginger.
3. In a large bowl, mix together the beef, cabbage, and green onions.
4. Divide the mixture into 6-8 portions and shape into patties.
5. Thread the beef and cabbage patties onto the bamboo skewers.
6. Place the skewers onto a foil-lined baking sheet and brush with the teriyaki glaze.
7. Broil for 15-20 minutes, flipping once and brushing with more glaze during cooking.

Nutrition Information(per serving): Calories 334, Total Fat 15.2g, Saturated Fat 5.5g, Cholesterol 79mg, Sodium 1090mg, Total Carbohydrates 19.3g, Dietary Fiber 2.1g, Sugars 10.7g, Protein 26.2g

36. Dijon Mustard Beef Kabobs

These Dijon Mustard Beef Kabobs are a delicious twist on traditional beef kabobs, marinated in a homemade Dijon Mustard sauce, perfect for grilling up on the BBQ.
Serving: 4
Preparation Time: 25 minutes
Ready Time: 30 minutes

Ingredients:
-1 tsp. olive oil
-1 clove garlic, minced
-2 Tbsp. Dijon mustard
-2 Tbsp. honey
-1/4 tsp. ground black pepper

-1 lb. lean beef, cubed
-1/2 onion, diced
-1 bell pepper, diced
-2 zucchini, sliced
-4 wooden skewers, soaked in water for 10 minutes

Instructions:
1. In a small bowl, whisk together olive oil, garlic, Dijon mustard, honey, and pepper.
2. Place beef cubes in a shallow dish and pour Dijon mustard mixture over top. Toss to coat. Cover and refrigerate for 15 minutes.
3. Preheat grill to medium-high heat.
4. Assemble kabobs by threading beef cubes, onion, bell pepper, and zucchini onto the skewers.
5. Place skewers onto the grill and cook for 10-15 minutes, turning occasionally, until beef is cooked through.

Nutrition Information: Per Serving: Calories: 161, Fat: 6.1 g, Carbohydrate: 9.5 g, Protein: 19.3 g, Sodium: 283 mg

37. Beef and Corn on the Cob Skewers

Beef and Corn on the Cob Skewers
Serving: 6
Preparation Time: 5 minutes
Ready Time: 15 minutes

Ingredients:
-1 1/2 pounds beef steak, cut into 1-inch cubes
-2 tablespoons olive oil
-1 tablespoon garlic powder
-1/2 teaspoon onion powder
-1/4 teaspoon smoked paprika
-6 ears of corn, husked
-Kosher salt and black pepper

Instructions:
1. Preheat the grill to medium heat.

2. In a large bowl, combine the beef cubes, olive oil, garlic powder, onion powder, and smoked paprika. Season with salt and pepper, then toss to coat.

3. Thread the beef cubes onto metal skewers, making sure to leave a little room for the corn later.

4. Place the skewers on the preheated grill. Grill for 7 to 8 minutes, flipping halfway through, or until the beef is cooked to your desired doneness.

5. Remove the skewers from the grill onto a plate, then thread the husked corn ears onto the skewers as well. Grill for 8 minutes, flipping halfway through, or until the corn is charred and cooked to your desired doneness.

6. Serve immediately.

Nutrition Information:
Calories: 174 kcal, Carbohydrates: 8 g, Protein: 15 g, Fat: 8 g, Saturated Fat: 2 g, Cholesterol: 40 mg, Sodium: 51 mg, Potassium: 329 mg, Fiber: 2 g, Sugar: 3 g, Vitamin A: 157 IU, Vitamin C: 9 mg, Calcium: 9 mg, Iron: 1 mg

38. Tandoori Spiced Beef Skewers

Tandoori spices are an amazing blend of flavors and aromas that make any dish stand out. Bring that amazing flavor to your next dinner with these tender and juicy Tandoori Spiced Beef Skewers!
Serving: 4
Preparation Time: 15 Minutes
Ready Time: 25 Minutes

Ingredients:
• 1 lb. beef tenderloin, cubed
• 2 tbsp. Tandoori Spice Mix
• 2 tsp. olive oil
•Salt and peppers to taste

Instructions:
1. Preheat your oven to 350°F and line a baking sheet with foil.

2. In a bowl, mix together the Tandoori Spice Mix, olive oil, salt and pepper.
3. Toss the cubed beef in the spice mixture until the beef is thoroughly coated.
4. Thread the cubed beef onto skewers and place on the prepared baking sheet.
5. Bake in the preheated oven for 25 minutes or until the beef is cooked through.

Nutrition Information per Serving: • Calories: 310
• Fat: 10g
• Carbs: 4g
• Protein: 45g

39. Beef and Radish Skewers

Beef and Radish Skewers are an easy and tasty meal the whole family will love. It is a simple combination of beef, radish, and spices all put together onto skewers and cooked to perfection.
Serving
Serves 4
Preparation Time
15 minutes
Ready Time
30 minutes

Ingredients:
- 8 beef cubes
- 8 radishes
- 1 tablespoon of olive oil
- 1 teaspoon of smoked paprika
- ½ teaspoon of chili flakes
- ½ teaspoon of garlic powder
- 4 wooden skewers

Instructions:
1. Preheat the oven to 375°F (190°C).
2. Cut the beef into cubes and the radishes into wedges.

3. Place the beef cubes and radish wedges on a baking tray.
4. Drizzle the olive oil over the beef and radish mixture.
5. Sprinkle the paprika, chili flakes, and garlic powder over the mixture.
6. Place the wooden skewers into the beef and radish mixture.
7. Bake in the preheated oven for 25-30 minutes, until the beef and radish are cooked through.

Nutrition Information
Per serving: 164 calories; 10.4 g fat; 0 g cholesterol; 327 mg sodium; 8.7 g carbohydrate; 2.3 g fiber; 12.3 g protein.

40. Smoky BBQ Beef Kabobs with Chipotle

Smoky BBQ Beef Kabobs with Chipotle are an easy, classic meal for summer barbecues or easy weeknight dinner.
Serving: 4
Preparation Time: 15 minutes
Ready Time: 40 minutes

Ingredients:
1 pound beef sirloin steak, cut into 1-inch cubes
1/4 cup olive oil
1/4 cup BBQ sauce
1 tablespoon lime juice
2 teaspoons chipotle chili pepper
1/2 teaspoon smoked paprika
1/4 teaspoon garlic powder
1/2 teaspoon cumin
1/2 teaspoon salt
2 green bell peppers, cut into 1-inch squares
1 red onion, cut into wedges

Instructions:
1. Preheat your grill to medium-high heat.
2. In a medium bowl, combine the oil, BBQ sauce, lime juice, chipotle chili pepper, smoked paprika, garlic powder, cumin, and salt. Add the cubed beef and mix to combine.
3. Thread the beef, bell pepper, and onion onto skewers.

4. Place the kabobs on the preheated grill and cook for 8-10 minutes, flipping halfway through, until the beef is cooked to your desired doneness.

Nutrition Information: 250 calories, 10g fat, 10g protein, 24g carbohydrates, 4g dietary fiber, 8g sugar.

41. Beef and Beet Skewers

Beef and Beet Skewers – A delicious and easy to make main course that combines the meaty flavor of beef with the sweetness of beets.
Serving: 4-6
Preparation Time: 10 minutes
Ready Time: 30 minutes

Ingredients:
- 1 lb of beef (sirloin, ribeye, or tenderloin), cut into 1-inch cubes
- 1 lb of small red beets, peeled and cut into ½-inch cubes
- 2 tablespoons olive oil
- 2 garlic cloves, minced
- 2 tablespoons smoked paprika
- 1 teaspoon dried oregano
- Salt and freshly ground black pepper, to taste
- 8 (6-inch) wooden skewers, soaked in water for 30 minutes

Instructions:
1. Preheat a grill or a grill pan to medium heat.
2. In a large bowl, combine the beef, beets, olive oil, garlic, paprika, and oregano. Toss to coat.
3. Season with salt and pepper, to taste.
4. Thread the beef and beet cubes onto the skewers, alternating between the two.
5. Grill the skewers, turning occasionally, for about 10 minutes, or until the beef and beets are cooked through.
6. Serve the skewers immediately.

Nutrition Information:

Calories: 172, Fat: 7.3g, Saturated fat: 2.2g, Carbohydrates: 7.7g, Sugar: 5.1g, Protein: 14.1g, Fiber: 2.7g, Cholesterol: 39mg, Sodium: 108mg.

42. Korean BBQ Beef Skewers with Gochujang

Korean BBQ Beef Skewers with Gochujang is a delicious, umami-rich barbecue dish made with marinated beef skewers, Gochujang (Korean chili paste) garlic oil, and toasted sesame seeds. It is easy to make and can be served as an appetizer or main dish.
Serving: 4
Preparation Time: 15 minutes
Ready Time: 20 minutes

Ingredients:
- 1 lb beef, cut into 1-inch cubes
- 3 tablespoons gochujang (Korean chili paste)
- 3 tablespoons garlic oil
- 2 tablespoons sesame seeds

Instructions:
1. Preheat the grill to medium-high heat.
2. Skewer the beef cubes onto bamboo or metal skewers.
3. In a small bowl, mix together the gochujang, garlic oil, and sesame seeds.
4. Brush the marinade onto the beef skewers.
5. Grill the beef skewers over the medium-high heat for about 8-10 minutes, turning periodically to ensure even cooking.
6. Remove from the grill and serve hot.

Nutrition Information (per serving):
Calories: 256 kcal
Protein: 23 g
Fat: 16 g
Carbohydrates: 5 g
Sodium: 166 mg

43. Beef and Avocado Skewers

Beef and Avocado Skewers
This delicious combination of beef and avocado skewered together is a tasty and easy way to make a meal. Perfect for a light dinner or even as an appetizer, these skewers are sure to be a hit.
Serving: 4
Preparation Time: 15 minutes
Ready Time: 20 minutes

Ingredients:
• 1/2 lb lean beef, cut into cubes
• 2 avocados, cut into cubes
• 1/3 cup balsamic vinegar
• 1 tablespoon olive oil
• 1 teaspoon garlic powder
• 1 teaspoon paprika
• Salt and pepper to taste

Instructions:
1. Preheat oven to 400 degrees F.
2. In a bowl, combine balsamic vinegar, olive oil, garlic powder, paprika, salt and pepper.
3. Add diced beef and avocado cubes and mix to coat.
4. Skewer beef and avocado cubes.
5. Place skewers on a baking sheet and bake for 15-20 minutes or until beef is cooked through.
6. Serve with desired sides and enjoy!

Nutrition Information:
Calories: 252, Fat: 15.2g, Cholesterol: 50mg, Sodium: 124mg, Carbohydrates: 10.6g, Protein: 19.2g, Fiber: 5g

44. Ginger Soy Beef Kabobs

Ginger Soy Beef Kabobs: Juicy kabobs of beef marinated in a ginger soy sauce, perfect for summer grilling and barbecue parties.
Serving: 6–8

Preparation Time: 15 minutes
Ready Time: 30 minutes

Ingredients:
• 2 tablespoons grated fresh ginger
• 1/2 cup soy sauce
• 2 tablespoons honey
• 2 garlic cloves, minced
• 1 tablespoon rice vinegar
• 2 tablespoons sesame oil
• 2 pounds top sirloin, cut into 1-inch cubes
• 1 red bell pepper, cut into 1-inch cubes
• 8 bamboo skewers, soaked in water

Instructions:
1. In a small bowl, mix together the ginger, soy sauce, honey, garlic, rice vinegar and sesame oil. Place the beef cubes into the marinade, tossing to evenly coat. Cover and let marinate for at least 30 minutes.
2. Preheat an outdoor grill for medium-high heat. Thread the beef cubes and pepper cubes onto the bamboo skewers.
3. Grill the kabobs for 4 to 5 minutes per side, or until the beef is cooked to desired doneness.

Nutrition Information:
• Calories: 284 kcal
• Protein: 28 g
• Fat: 9 g
• Carbohydrates: 7 g
• Sodium: 1940 mg
• Fiber: 1 g
• Sugar: 5 g

45. Beef and Brussels Sprouts Skewers

Delicious and savory, Beef and Brussels Sprouts Skewers are an easy and healthy dinner option.
Serving: 4
Preparation Time: 20 minutes

Ready Time: 40 minutes

Ingredients:
- 1 pound lean beef sirloin, cut into cubes
- 2 tablespoons olive oil
- 2 teaspoons garlic, minced
- 2 teaspoons ground oregano
- Salt and pepper to taste
- 2 cups Brussels sprouts, trimmed and cut in half
- 8 metal or bamboo skewers

Instructions:
1. Preheat the oven to 400 F.
2. Soak the metal or bamboo skewers in water for 20 minutes.
3. In a large bowl, combine the beef cubes, olive oil, garlic, oregano, salt, and pepper.
4. Mix well to combine.
5. Thread the beef cubes and Brussels sprouts onto the skewers.
6. Arrange the skewers on a baking sheet lined with parchment paper.
7. Bake in the preheated oven for 20 minutes.
8. Serve hot.

Nutrition Information:
Each serving contains approximately: 248 calories, 14.5g fat, 6.4g saturated fat, 57.9g protein, 4.6g carbohydrates, and 2.9g dietary fiber.

46. Moroccan Beef Kabobs with Harissa

Moroccan Beef Kabobs with Harissa
Serving: 4
Preparation Time: 15 minutes
Ready Time: 20 minutes

Ingredients:
1 large onion, cut into 1-inch pieces
1 lb (450 g) lean beef cubed into 1-inch pieces
3 tablespoons olive oil
1 teaspoon garlic powder

2 teaspoons cumin
2 teaspoons paprika
1 teaspoon cinnamon
1/4 teaspoon cayenne pepper
1 teaspoon dried oregano
Salt and black pepper, for seasoning
2 tablespoons harissa sauce

Instructions:
1. Preheat the oven to 400 degrees F (200 degrees C).
2. In a large bowl mix together the beef cubes, olive oil, garlic powder, cumin, paprika, cinnamon, cayenne pepper, oregano, salt and pepper until the beef cubes are entirely coated with the spices.
3. On 8 wooden or metal skewers, alternate onions and beef cubes until each skewer is filled.
4. Place the skewers onto a baking sheet and bake for 18-20 minutes, or until the beef is cooked to desired doneness.
5. Brush the skewers with harissa sauce and serve.

Nutrition Information:
Calories: 210 kcal, Carbohydrates: 6 g, Protein: 18 g, Fat: 11 g, Saturated Fat: 2 g, Cholesterol: 45 mg, Sodium: 268 mg, Potassium: 356 mg, Fiber: 1 g, Sugar: 2 g, Vitamin A: 363 IU, Vitamin C: 5 mg, Calcium: 29 mg, Iron: 3 mg

47. Beef and Swiss Chard Skewers

Enjoy a savory and nutritious meal with these skewers of beef and Swiss chard. The beef is flavored with rosemary, garlic, and oregano for a hearty flavor, while the Swiss chard adds a bright and tasty complement.
Serving: 4
Preparation Time: 15 mins
Ready Time: 35 mins

Ingredients:
- 1 pound 95% lean ground beef
- 1 large head of Swiss chard (leaves and stalks), washed and chopped
- 2 teaspoons minced garlic

- 1 teaspoon fresh oregano, chopped
- 1 teaspoon fresh rosemary, finely chopped
- Salt and black pepper to taste
- 2 tablespoons extra-virgin olive oil

Instructions:
1. Preheat your grill to high heat.
2. In a large bowl, combine the ground beef, garlic, oregano, rosemary, salt, and pepper together with your hands. Work the mixture until everything is evenly distributed.
3. Grab small pieces of the mixture in your hands, around 2 tablespoons, and form into flat, elongated shapes. Thread the beef onto each skewer, alternating with one piece of chard (or two, depending on the size).
4. Brush the skewers lightly with olive oil to help prevent sticking. Place them on the grill. Cook for about 7-8 minutes, flipping and continuing to brush with olive oil as needed.
5. When the beef is cooked through, remove the skewers from the grill and enjoy!

Nutrition Information:
Serving size: 1 skewer
Calories: 140
Fat: 5g
Carbohydrates: 4g
Protein: 20g

48. Teriyaki Beef and Pineapple Kabobs

This delicious dish brings together tender teriyaki-seasoned beef cubes, pineapple chunks, and peppers all skewered together and grilled for a quick, easy meal.
Serving: Makes 4 servings
Preparation Time: 10 minutes
Ready Time: 15 minutes

Ingredients:
1 Lb. lean beef cubes
1/2 cup teriyaki sauce

1 red bell pepper, cut into chunks
1 green bell pepper, cut into chunks
1/2 of a fresh pineapple, cut into chunks

Instructions:
1. Thread the beef cubes, bell peppers, and pineapple chunks onto metal skewers until all of the Ingredients have been used.
2. Place the skewers onto a greased grill over medium-high heat.
3. Brush the teriyaki sauce onto the skewers and cook until the beef cubes are cooked through, about 7-10 minutes, turning and brushing with more teriyaki sauce as needed.

Nutrition Information:
Calories: 280, Protein: 23g, Fat: 9g, Sodium: 1066mg, Carbohydrates: 23g, Sugar: 17g.

49. Beef and Butternut Squash Skewers

Enjoy this delicious dish of beef and Butternut Squash Skewers. It is a great way to get your daily dose of protein and vegetables in a tasty and easy package. This dish will make an excellent side dish or main course.
Serving: 4
Preparation Time: 15 minutes
Ready Time: 30 minutes

Ingredients:
-1 Butternut Squash, cut into 1 1/2 inch cubes
-1lb beef cube steak, cut into 1 inch cubes
-1 tablespoon olive oil
-Salt and pepper, to taste
-1 teaspoon garlic powder
-1/4 teaspoon cumin
-1/4 teaspoon oregano
-1/4 teaspoon smoked paprika

Instructions:
1. Preheat oven to 400 degrees F (200 degrees C).

2. In a large bowl, combine the butternut squash cubes, beef cubes, olive oil, salt, pepper, garlic powder, cumin, oregano, and smoked paprika.
3. Mix together until evenly combined.
4. Thread the beef cubes and butternut squash cubes onto skewers.
5. Place skewers onto a baking sheet lined with foil.
6. Bake for 20-25 minutes or until beef is cooked through and the squash has softened.
7. Serve warm with your favorite sides and enjoy.

Nutrition Information:
Serving Size: 1 skewer
Calories: 141
Total Fat: 4.3 g
Saturated Fat: 1.2 g
Cholesterol: 33 mg
Sodium: 100 mg
Potassium: 408 mg
Total Carbohydrate: 11 g
Dietary Fiber: 2 g
Sugars: 4 g
Protein: 13.1 g

50. Italian Beef Skewers with Tomatoes and Basil

Italian Beef Skewers with Tomatoes and Basil
Serving: 4
Preparation time: 15 minutes
Ready Time: 25 minutes

Ingredients:
• 1 1/3 pounds of beef chuck
• 2 tablespoons of EVOO
• 2 cloves of garlic minced
• 2 teaspoons of dried oregano
• 1 teaspoon of salt
• 1 teaspoon of pepper
• 1 pint of cherry tomatoes
• 1/4 cup of fresh basil leaves

Instructions:
1. Cut beef chuck into 1-inch cubes and place them in a large bowl.
2. Combine EVOO, garlic, oregano, salt, and pepper in a small bowl and mix well.
3. Pour the mixture over the beef cubes and toss to coat evenly.
4. Thread the beef cubes onto metal skewers, alternating with the tomatoes.
5. Heat a grill to medium-high, or preheat a skillet over medium-high heat.
6. Grill or sauté the skewers for 6-7 minutes per side, or until the beef cubes are cooked.
7. Transfer the skewers to a plate and garnish with fresh basil leaves.

Nutrition Information:
• 119 Calories
• 7.6g Fat
• 3.2g Carbs
• 10.3g Protein

51. Beef and Radicchio Skewers

Beef and Radicchio Skewers is a unique and flavorful appetizer that combines the robust taste of beef with the mild bitterness of radicchio. This dish is perfect for serving at group gatherings or as a light meal.
Serving: 4-6
Preparation time: 10 minutes
Ready time: 25 minutes

Ingredients:
-1 lb beef sirloin, cut into cubes
-1 head radicchio, cut into cubes
-2 tablespoons olive oil
-1/2 teaspoon garlic powder
-1/2 teaspoon paprika
-1/4 teaspoon salt
-1/4 teaspoon ground black pepper

Instructions:
1. Preheat the oven to 350 F.
2. Place the beef and radicchio cubes on wooden skewers.
3. In a large bowl, combine the olive oil, garlic powder, paprika, salt, and ground black pepper.
4. Brush the skewers with the olive oil mixture.
5. Place the skewers on a greased baking sheet.
6. Bake in preheated oven for 20 minutes, turning the skewers over after 10 minutes.
7. Serve and enjoy.

Nutrition Information:
Serving Size: 1 skewer
Calories: 122 calories
Fat: 7.4 g
Carbohydrates: 4.8 g
Protein: 9.2 g

52. Greek-Style Beef Skewers with Tzatziki Sauce

Greek-Style Beef Skewers with Tzatziki Sauce is a flavorful and satisfying dish that is perfect for any special occasion. This dish consists of kebabs of beef infused with Greek flavors, and served with a homemade Tzatziki sauce. This dish can be served as a main course or an appetizer, and is sure to please Greek food lovers.
Serving: 4-6
Preparation Time: 25 minutes
Ready Time: 25 minutes

Ingredients:
- 1 pound Beef Skirt Steak, cut into 1 inch cubes
- 2 cloves Garlic, minced
- 1/4 cup Olive Oil
- 1/4 cup Red Wine Vinegar
- 2 teaspoons of chopped fresh Oregano
- Salt and Black Pepper, to taste
Tzatziki Sauce:
- 1 cup Greek-Style Plain Yogurt

- 1/4 cucumber, finely shredded
- 1 tablespoon fresh Lemon Juice
- 1 teaspoon freshly chopped Dill
- Salt and Black Pepper to taste

Instructions:
1. Start by preparing the marinade for the beef. In a bowl, whisk together the garlic, oil, vinegar, oregano, salt, and pepper to make the marinade.
2. Place the beef cubes into a resealable plastic bag and add the marinade. Seal the bag and massage the beef until the marinade is evenly distributed. Refrigerate for at least 20 minutes (or up to overnight).
3. To prepare the Tzatziki Sauce, stir together the yogurt, cucumber, lemon juice, dill, salt, and pepper in a bowl until combined.
4. When ready to cook, preheat a grill to medium-high heat.
5. Thread the marinaded beef onto skewers and grill for about 5 minutes, turning once, until the beef is cooked through.
6. Serve the beef skewers with the Tzatziki Sauce.

Nutrition Information:
Calories: 260; Protein: 21g; Fat: 15g; Carbs: 3g; Sodium: 125mg; Sugar: 2g

53. Beef and Kabocha Squash Skewers

Beef and Kabocha Squash Skewers
Serving: 4
Preparation Time: 20 minutes
Ready Time: 50 minutes

Ingredients:
- 1 kabocha squash, cut into 1-inch cubes
- 1 pound beef top round, cut into 1-inch cubes
- 2 tablespoons olive oil
- 2 tablespoons fresh rosemary, chopped
- 2 teaspoons garlic powder
- 1 teaspoon onion powder
- Salt and pepper, to taste

Instructions:
1. Preheat outdoor grill or indoor grill pan to medium heat.
2. In a medium bowl, combine the squash, beef cubes, olive oil, rosemary, garlic powder, onion powder, salt, and pepper. Toss until all Ingredients are well combined.
3. Start assembling the skewers with a piece of beef and squash, followed by another piece of beef and squash. Alternate until all the Ingredients have been used.
4. Grill the skewers for 20 minutes, flipping each skewer every 5 minutes.

Nutrition Information:
Calories: 191 kcal, Carbohydrates: 9 g, Protein: 20 g, Fat: 8 g, Saturated Fat: 2 g, Cholesterol: 46 mg, Sodium: 81 mg, Potassium: 536 mg, Fiber: 2 g, Sugar: 3 g, Vitamin A: 380 IU, Vitamin C: 24 mg, Calcium: 37 mg, Iron: 2 mg.

54. Honey Soy Glazed Beef Kabobs

Honey Soy Glazed Beef Kabobs
Serving: 4
Preparation Time: 10 minutes
Ready Time: 20 minutes

Ingredients:
- 1/4 Cup Low-Sodium Soy Sauce
- 2 tablespoons Honey
- 1 Garlic Clove (minced)
- 1 teaspoon Crushed Red Pepper
- 1/2 teaspoon Ground Ginger
- 2 tablespoons Vegetable Oil
- 1 Pound Beef (cut into 1.5 inch cubes)
- Bell Pepper And Onion (cut into cubes, use equal amounts)

Instructions:
1. Preheat your grill for medium-high heat. Spray the kabob skewers with cooking spray or brush with oil.
2. In a small bowl, mix together soy sauce, honey, garlic, crushed red pepper, ground ginger, and vegetable oil to create a marinade.

3. Place the cubed beef and vegetables into the marinade and stir to coat. Allow the mixture to sit for 5 minutes.
4. Begin threading the beef and vegetables on to the kabob skewers, alternating between the two.
5. Place the kabobs onto the preheated grill. Cook for 10 minutes, turning occasionally, and basting with remaining marinade.

Nutrition Information:
Calories: 303, Total Fat: 17 g, Saturated Fat: 4 g, Sodium: 925 mg, Carbohydrates: 11 g, Protein: 26 g

55. Beef and Cherry Pepper Skewers

Beef and Cherry Pepper Skewers
Serving: 4
Preparation time: 15 minutes
Ready time: 25 minutes

Ingredients:
1 ½ cups beef, cut into cubes
3 tablespoons olive oil
½ cup balsamic vinegar
2 cloves garlic, finely grated
½ teaspoon sea salt
2 cups yellow bell pepper, cut into 1-inch cubes
2 cups cherry pepper, cut into 1-inch cubes
2 tablespoons fresh parsley, cut

Instructions:
1. In a medium bowl, mix the beef cubes, olive oil, balsamic vinegar, garlic, and sea salt together.
2. Skewer the beef cubes alternating with the bell pepper cubes and the cherry pepper cubes.
3. Grill the skewers on medium-high heat for about 10 minutes until the beef is cooked through, turning occasionally.
4. Remove the skewers from the grill and sprinkle with parsley before serving.

Nutrition Information:
Calories: 190
Total Fat: 11g
Carbohydrates: 6g
Protein: 14g
These delicious and savory Beef and Cherry Pepper Skewers make a great main course or appetizer for any occasion. Made with beef cubes, balsamic vinegar, garlic, bell peppers, and cherry peppers, they are grilled to perfection! Serve with some fresh parsley and enjoy these flavorful skewers!

56. Spanish-Style Beef and Chorizo Skewers

Get ready for a mouth-watering meal with these Spanish-Style Beef and Chorizo Skewers! Perfect for the grill or a weeknight dinner, these tasty skewers are full of flavor, and sure to be a crowd-pleaser.
Serving: Serves 6
Preparation Time: 15 minutes
Ready Time: 25 minutes

Ingredients:
• 2 lbs. beef sirloin, cubed
• 1 chorizo, cut into small slices
• 3 large bell peppers, chopped
• 1 white onion, chopped
• Olive oil
• 2 cloves garlic, minced
• 2 teaspoons paprika
• 1 teaspoon oregano
• 2 tablespoons lemon juice
• Salt and pepper, to taste

Instructions:
1. Preheat grill or oven to 400 degrees.
2. In a large bowl, combine beef cubes, chorizo, bell pepper, and onion.
3. Add olive oil, garlic, paprika, oregano, lemon juice, salt, and pepper, mixing to combine.

4. Thread the beef and vegetables onto skewers, alternating the Ingredients.
5. Grill on preheated grill or bake in preheated oven for 15-20 minutes, turning occasionally, or until beef is cooked through.

Nutrition Information: Calories: 285; Total Fat: 14g; Saturated Fat: 4.9g; Cholesterol: 66.5mg; Sodium: 360.1mg; Carbohydrates: 11.1g; Sugar: 2.5g; Fiber: 2.2g; Protein: 28.1g.

57. Beef and Nectarine Skewers

Beef and Nectarine Skewers
Serving: 4
Preparation time: 20 minutes
Ready time: 25 minutes

Ingredients:
• 2 tablespoons extra-virgin olive oil
• 2 tablespoons balsamic vinegar
• Salt and freshly ground black pepper
• 2 tablespoons chopped fresh mint
• 1/2 pound skirt steak, cut into 1-inch cubes
• 2 large nectarines, cut into 1-inch cubes

Instructions:
1. In a large bowl, whisk together the olive oil, balsamic vinegar, salt and pepper.
2. Add the mint and steak cubes to the bowl and toss to coat. Let marinate for 10 minutes.
3. Thread the steak cubes and nectarine cubes onto 8 skewers.
4. Grill or broil the skewers for 5 minutes per side, or until the steak is cooked to desired doneness.

Nutrition Information:
Calories: 154, Fat: 6g, Cholesterol: 36mg, Sodium: 103mg, Carbohydrates: 9g, Fiber: 2g, Protein: 14g

58. Vietnamese-Style Beef Skewers with Nuoc Cham Sauce

This easy Vietnamese-Style Beef Skewers with Nuoc Cham Sauce dish is full of flavor and perfect for summer grilling. It's simple to make and comes together in no time.

Serving: 4
Preparation Time: 10 minutes
Ready Time: 20 minutes

Ingredients:
-1/3 cup of fresh lime juice
-1/3 cup of fish sauce
-2 tablespoons of sugar
-2 tablespoons of water
-2 garlic cloves, minced
-1/4 teaspoon of crushed red pepper flakes
-1 lb of beef sirloin steak, cut into 1-inch cubes
-1 teaspoon of freshly ground black pepper
-1/2 teaspoon of paprika
-4 wooden skewers, soaked in water for 30 minutes

Instructions:
1. In a medium bowl, whisk together the lime juice, fish sauce, sugar, water, garlic, and red pepper flakes. Set aside.
2. Preheat the grill or broiler to medium-high heat.
3. In a large bowl, mix together the beef cubes, pepper, and paprika.
4. Thread 4 cubes onto each skewer.
5. Grill or broil the beef skewers, turning occasionally, for about 8 to 10 minutes until cooked to desired doneness.
6. Brush the Nuoc Cham Sauce onto the beef skewers as they cook.
7. Serve hot with remaining Nuoc Cham Sauce on the side, if desired.

Nutrition Information: Per Serving: Calories 337, Fat 13.3 g (Saturated 5.3 g, Trans 0 g), Cholesterol 82 mg, Sodium 941 mg, Carbs 11.5 g (Fiber 0.2 g, Sugars 9.4 g), Protein 36.1 g.

59. Beef and Okra Skewers

Spicy, savory and bold — these Beef and Okra Skewers are sure to please! Featuring delicious, simple Ingredients and easy preparation, these skewers are quick and easy enough to prepare during your busiest nights.

Serving: 6
Preparation Time: 30 minutes
Ready Time: 30 minutes

Ingredients:

-2 tablespoons paprika
-1 1/2 teaspoons smoked paprika
-1 teaspoon ground cumin
-1 teaspoon garlic powder
-1/2 teaspoon dried oregano
-1/2 teaspoon freshly cracked pepper
-1/4 teaspoon kosher salt
-1 tablespoon olive oil
-1 1/4 lb sirloin or top round steak, cut into 1-inch cubes
-2 large bell peppers, any color, cut into 1-inch squares
-1 lb frozen okra
-6 metal or wooden skewers

Instructions:

1. Preheat your grill to medium-high heat.
2. In a small bowl, mix together the paprika, smoked paprika, cumin, garlic powder, oregano, cracked pepper and kosher salt. Set aside.
3. In a medium bowl, combine the olive oil with the cubed steak and the bell pepper squares. Use your hands to mix to combine.
4. Place 1/4 cup of the seasoning mixture in the bowl and mix until the steak and peppers are evenly coated.
5. Thread the steak and bell peppers onto the skewers. Alternate the beef and bell peppers.
6. Grill the skewers for 8-10 minutes, turning occasionally, until the steak has reached desired doneness.
7. Arrange the okra on a baking sheet and sprinkle with the remaining seasoning mixture.

8. Place the baking sheet of okra on the lowest rack of the preheated grill. Roast for 10 minutes, stirring occasionally, until the okra is tender and lightly charred.
9. Serve the beef and okra skewers with the grilled okra.

Nutrition Information: one serving contains 250 calories, 16g fat, 8g carbohydrates, 20g protein, and 500mg of sodium.

60. Maple Bourbon Glazed Beef Kabobs

Maple Bourbon Glazed Beef Kabobs are an easy and flavorful grilling entrée that is perfect for a spring or summer day. This delicious recipe combines beef, sweet maple syrup and a touch of flavorful bourbon together for a burger alternative with an unforgettable flavor.
Serving: 4
Preparation time: 10 minutes
Ready time: 20 minutes

Ingredients:
- 2 tablespoons Dijon mustard
- 1/4 cup bourbon
- 1/4 cup maple syrup
- 1 tablespoon garlic powder
- 1 tablespoon dried parsley
- 1 teaspoon chili powder
- 1 teaspoon onion powder
- 1/2 teaspoon smoked paprika
- Salt and pepper, to taste
- 1 1/2 lbs. beef kabob cubes
- 4 wooden skewers

Instructions:
1. In a bowl whisk together Dijon mustard, bourbon, maple syrup, garlic powder, dried parsley, chili powder, onion powder, smoked paprika, and salt and pepper.
2. Place the beef cubes in a large bowl and toss the kabobs with the bourbon glaze.
3. Thread the beef cubes onto the four glued skewers.

4. Preheat your grill and once the coals are ashed over evenly place the skewers on the grates. Allow the kabobs to cook for 7 to 8 minutes turning the once or twice during cooking time.
5. Remove the kabobs from the grill and serve hot.

Nutrition Information (per serving):
Calories: 300
Total Fat: 16g
Saturated Fat: 6g
Cholesterol: 78mg
Sodium: 296mg
Total Carbohydrates: 12g
Dietary Fiber: 0g
Sugars: 9g
Protein: 26g

61. Beef and Swiss Cheese Skewers

Beef and Swiss Cheese Skewers - Enjoy these delicious bite-sized skewers made with beef cubes and Swiss cheese for a tasty and easy appetizer.

Serving: 4
Preparation Time: 10 minutes
Ready Time: 15 minutes

Ingredients:
- 1 pound beef cubes
- 8 ounces Swiss cheese, cubed
- 2 tablespoons olive oil
- 1 teaspoon garlic powder
- 1 teaspoon oregano
- 1 teaspoon smoked paprika
- ¼ teaspoon freshly ground black pepper
- Salt to taste

Instructions:
1. Preheat oven to 350°F.

2. In a bowl, combine the olive oil, garlic powder, oregano, smoked paprika, and black pepper.
3. Marinate the beef cubes in the olive oil mixture for 10 minutes.
4. Thread the beef cubes and Swiss cheese onto skewers.
5. Place the skewers on a baking sheet.
6. Bake for 15 minutes, or until the beef is cooked through.
7. Serve warm.

Nutrition Information:
Per serving: 266 calories, 14 g fat, 17 g protein, 7 g carbohydrates, 0 g dietary fiber, 0 g sugar, 150 mg cholesterol, 744 mg sodium.

62. Moroccan-Spiced Beef and Quince Skewers

This delicious recipe of Moroccan-Spiced Beef and Quince Skewers will give you a taste of the exotic. Combining flavorful seasoned beef with sweet, juicy, and tart quince will make for a balanced meal.
Serving: Serves 4
Preparation Time: 15 minutes
Ready Time: 30 minutes

Ingredients:
• ¼ cup olive oil
• 2 cloves garlic, minced
• 1½ teaspoons sweet paprika
• 1 teaspoon ground cumin
• ½ teaspoon ground coriander
• ½ teaspoon freshly ground black pepper
• 1 teaspoon kosher salt
• 1 pound lean ground beef
• 4 wooden skewers
• 2 large quince, cut into 1-inch cubes

Instructions:
1. In a medium bowl, whisk together the olive oil, minced garlic, sweet paprika, ground cumin, ground coriander, freshly ground black pepper, and kosher salt.

2. Add the lean ground beef to the bowl and mix the beef with the marinade until the Ingredients are evenly incorporated.

3. Let the beef marinate for at least 30 minutes or up to 24 hours.

4. Once the beef is marinated, thread pieces of the beef and cubes of quince onto each skewer, alternating between each ingredient.

5. Heat a grill over medium-high heat and lightly oil the grate.

6. Grill the kebabs for about 5 minutes per side, until the beef is cooked through and lightly charred.

7. Serve warm with a side of your favorite vegetables and grains.

Nutrition Information:
Calories: 443, Total Fat: 25.5 g, Saturated Fat: 8.2 g, Cholesterol: 92 mg, Sodium: 554 mg, Total Carbohydrate 20.8 g, Dietary Fiber: 3.8 g, Total Sugar: 7.8 g, Protein 26.7 g.

63. Beef and Celeriac Skewers

This is an easy and delicious recipe for Beef and Celeriac Skewers with a savory honey glaze.

Serving: 4

Preparation Time: 10 minutes

Ready Time: 20 minutes

Ingredients:
- 14 oz beef cut of choice diced into cubes
- 1 celeriac, cut into small cubes
- 2 tbsp honey
- 2 tbsp olive oil
- 1 tsp garlic powder
- 1/2 tsp chili powder
- Salt and pepper, to taste

Instructions:
1. Preheat the oven to 400°F.

2. Arrange the beef cubes and celeriac cubes on metal skewers alternatively. Place the skewers on a baking sheet.

3. In a small bowl, mix together the honey, olive oil, garlic powder and chili powder. Pour the glaze over the skewers. Season with salt and black pepper.
4. Bake in the oven for about 20 minutes or until the beef and celeriac cubes are cooked through.
5. Serve the skewers with your favorite side dish.

Nutrition Information:
Per serving:
Calories: 267, Total fat: 11 g, Saturated fat: 3g, Cholesterol: 68mg, Sodium: 156mg, Total carbohydrates: 17g, Dietary fiber: 4g, Sugar: 10g, Protein: 24g.

64. Lemon Garlic Beef Kabobs

A delicious beef dish prepared with simple Ingredients and great for summer grilling, Lemon Garlic Beef Kabobs are a crowd pleaser.
Serving: 4-6
Preparation Time: 15 minutes
Ready Time: 8 hours 30 minutes

Ingredients:
2 lbs sirloin steak, cut into 1-inch cubes
3 tablespoons olive oil
3 tablespoons lemon juice
3 cloves garlic, finely chopped
1 teaspoon dried oregano
Salt and pepper, to taste

Instructions:
1. In a large bowl combine the olive oil, lemon juice, garlic, oregano, salt, and pepper. Add the steak cubes and mix until coated. Cover the bowl and let the steak marinate in the refrigerator for at least 8 hours.
2. Preheat your outdoor grill or grill pan.
3. Once the steak is done marinating, remove it from the refrigerator and thread cubes of steak onto kabob sticks alternating them with cherry tomatoes if desired.

4. Grill the kabobs over medium-high heat for 8-10 minutes, turning periodically to make sure all sides are cooked evenly.

Nutrition Information: Each serving of Lemon Garlic Beef Kabobs contains approximately 227 calories, 14 g of fat, 19 g of protein, and 1 g of carbohydrates.

65. Beef and Mustard Greens Skewers

Beef and Mustard Greens Skewers are an Asian-inspired meal made up of tender beef marinated in a mix of soy sauce, garlic, green onion, and sesame oil, and then threaded onto skewers and cooked to perfection. Serves 4. Preparation Time: 15 minutes. Ready Time: 10-15 minutes.

Ingredients:
- 1 lbs of beef
- 2 cups of mustard greens
- 4 tablespoons of soy sauce
- 1 tablespoon of roasted sesame oil
- 1 teaspoon of garlic
- 1/2 cup of green onions
- 4 tablespoons of oil

Instructions:
1. In a medium bowl, combine the soy sauce, sesame oil, garlic, and green onions until well blended.
2. Place the beef into the bowl and stir until the beef is evenly coated in the marinade. Allow it to marinate for 10 minutes.
3. Thread the mustard greens and beef onto the skewers.
4. Heat a frying pan on medium-high heat with a tablespoon of oil.
5. Place the skewers onto the pan and cook for 10-15 minutes or until the beef is cooked through.
Nutrition Information: Calories: 247, Carbohydrates: 3g, Protein: 24g, Fat: 15g, Sodium: 741mg, Potassium: 445mg

66. Brazilian-Style Beef Skewers with Chimichurri Sauce

Brazilian-Style Beef Skewers with Chimichurri Sauce is a delicious Brazilian dish made with marinated beef skewers, onions, peppers, and a tasty chimichurri dipping sauce.
Serving: 8
Preparation Time: 10 minutes
Ready Time: 4 hours

Ingredients:
- 2 pounds of skirt steak, cut into 1-2 inch cubes
- 2 tablespoons of olive oil
- 2 teaspoons of dried oregano
- 1 teaspoon of garlic powder
- 2 teaspoons of smoked paprika
- 1 teaspoon of ground cumin
- 1 teaspoon of sea salt
- 1 teaspoon of freshly ground black pepper
- 1 large red onion, cut into 1-2 inch pieces
- 2 red bell peppers, cut into 1-2 inch pieces
- 4-6 wooden skewers
Chimichurri Sauce:
- 1 cup of chopped fresh parsley
- 2 cloves of garlic, minced
- 2 tablespoons of red wine vinegar
- juice of 1 large lemon
- 2 tablespoons of olive oil
- 1 teaspoon of dried oregano
- 1/4 teaspoon of sea salt

Instructions:
1. Start by mixing together the olive oil, oregano, garlic powder, smoked paprika, cumin, sea salt, and pepper in a bowl.
2. Add the steak cubes and mix until they are evenly coated. Cover and let marinate in the refrigerator for at least 4 hours.
3. Preheat the oven to 400 degrees F.
4. Thread the steak cubes, onions, and bell peppers onto the wooden skewers, alternating between each item.

5. Place the skewers onto a baking sheet lined with parchment paper and bake for 15-20 minutes, or until the steak is cooked through.
6. Meanwhile, make the chimichurri sauce by combining the parsley, garlic, red wine vinegar, lemon juice, olive oil, oregano, and sea salt in a food processor or blender and blend until smooth.
7. Serve the skewers with the chimichurri sauce and enjoy!

Nutrition Information:
Calories: 418 kcal, Carbohydrates: 9 g, Protein: 37 g, Fat: 25 g, Saturated Fat: 8 g, Monounsaturated Fat: 14 g, Cholesterol: 100 mg, Sodium: 867 mg, Potassium: 591 mg, Fiber: 2 g, Sugar: 3 g, Vitamin A: 1532 IU, Vitamin C: 59 mg, Calcium: 89 mg, Iron: 4 mg

67. Beef and Cucumber Skewers

Beef and Cucumber Skewers - This delicious and easy-to-make recipe is great for any party or gathering. Serve these succulent skewers with a dip of your choice for a perfect appetizer!
Serving: 4
Preparation Time: 10 minutes
Ready Time: 30 minutes

Ingredients:
- 500g beef sirloin cut into cubes
- 2 cucumbers cut into cubes
- 2 tablespoons olive oil
- 1 tablespoon sesame oil
- 2 tablespoons soy sauce
- 1 garlic clove, minced
- Salt and pepper to taste
- 4 wooden skewers

Instructions:
1. Preheat oven to 400 degrees F and line a baking sheet with parchment paper.
2. In a large bowl, combine the beef, cucumber cubes, olive oil, sesame oil, soy sauce, garlic, salt, and pepper. Mix until the Ingredients are completely combined.

3. Thread the beef and cucumber cubes onto the wooden skewers.
4. Place the skewers onto the prepared baking sheet and bake in the preheated oven for about 30 minutes, or until the beef is cooked through.
5. Serve hot with a dip of your choice.

Nutrition Information:
Calories: 250 kcal, Total Fat: 14.2 g, Total Carbohydrates: 8 g, Protein: 22.4 g

68. Jerk Beef and Plantain Skewers

Jerk Beef and Plantain Skewers – A flavorful Caribbean-inspired dish with tender beef and sweet plantains, these skewers are sure to please!
Serving: 4
Preparation Time: 10 minutes
Ready Time: 20 minutes

Ingredients:
• ½ lb. skirt steak, cut into cubes
• 2 tbsp olive oil
• 2 cloves garlic, finely minced
• 2 tsp dried oregano
• 2 tsp jerk seasoning
• 1 tsp fresh thyme, minced
• 2 large ripe plantains, peeled and cut into 1 inch chunks
• Skewers

Instructions:
1. In a large bowl, combine olive oil, garlic, oregano, jerk seasoning and thyme. Stir to combine. Add beef cubes and toss to coat. Allow to marinate in the refrigerator for about 10 minutes.
2. Heat a grill or a large grill pan over medium-high heat. Thread beef and plantain chunks onto skewers, alternating between beef and plantain.
3. Grill skewers for about 10-12 minutes, flipping half way through until beef is cooked through and plantains are browned. Serve warm.

Nutrition Information: (per serving)

- Calories: 299 kcal
- Protein: 22 g
- Fat: 16 g
- Carbs: 22 g

69. Beef and Kohlrabi Skewers

Beef and Kohlrabi Skewers
This easy to make dish is a perfect option to serve for any summer gathering. These colorful beef and kohlrabi skewers are sure to brighten up any meal.
Serving: 4
Preparation time: 10 minutes
Ready time: 25 minutes

Ingredients:
- 1 lb flank steak, cut into 1-inch cubes
- 4 medium kohlrabi, peeled and cut into 1-inch cubes
- 1/4 cup olive oil
- 2 tablespoons fresh thyme leaves
- 2 tablespoons freshly squeezed lemon juice
- 1 teaspoon Dijon mustard
- Salt and freshly ground black pepper

Instructions:
1. Preheat grill or broiler to medium-high heat.
2. In a large bowl, combine beef cubes, kohlrabi cubes, olive oil, thyme, lemon juice, and mustard. Toss to combine and season with salt and pepper.
3. Thread beef and kohlrabi onto metal or wooden skewers.
4. Place skewers on grill or broiler and cook for 10 minutes, turning once, until lightly charred and just cooked through.

Nutrition Information:
Serving size: 1 skewer
Calories: 133
Total Fat: 7.7g
Saturated Fat: 1.6g

Total Carbohydrate: 4.6g
Fiber: 3.2g
Sugar: 1.2g
Protein: 11.3g

70. Thai Red Curry Beef Skewers

Thai Red Curry Beef Skewers is a flavorful, tender and delicious dish packed with red curry paste, coconut milk, and lemon grass. Serves 4, with 10 minutes preparation time and 20 minutes ready time.

Ingredients:
- 1 lb beef, cut into thin slices
- 1 tbs of red curry paste
- 2 tbs of coconut milk
- 1 tbs of fish sauce
- 1 stalk of lemon grass, crushed
- 2 tbs of oil

Instructions:
1. In a bowl, mix the beef, red curry paste, coconut milk, fish sauce, and crushed lemon grass together.
2. Heat oil in a skillet over medium heat.
3. Add beef mixture and cook until beef is lightly browned and cooked through.
4. Place the beef onto skewers and serve.

Nutrition Information:
Calories: 333, Fat: 18g, Carbohydrates: 3g, Protein: 33g, Sodium: 587mg

71. Beef and Fennel Skewers

Beef and Fennel Skewers are a healthy and flavorful way to enjoy fresh vegetables. This particular recipe is so easy to make and packed with nutrition, thanks to lean ground beef and fresh fennel.
Serving: 4
Preparation time: 15 minutes

Ready time: 25 minutes

Ingredients:
- 1 lb. lean ground beef
- 1 large bulb of fennel, diced
- 2 cloves garlic, minced
- 2 tablespoons olive oil
- 2 tablespoons red wine vinegar
- 1 teaspoon Italian seasoning
- Salt and pepper, to taste

Instructions:
1. Preheat the oven to 400°F.
2. In a medium bowl, combine the ground beef, diced fennel, garlic, olive oil, red wine vinegar, Italian seasoning, salt, and pepper. Mix everything together and form into small balls.
3. Line a baking sheet with parchment paper and spray with cooking spray. Using a skewer, thread a meatball onto each skewer. Place on the baking sheet and bake for 20 minutes.
4. Serve the skewers hot, with a fresh side salad.

Nutrition Information (per serving):
Calories: 280, Fat: 18g, Cholesterol: 55mg, Sodium: 145mg, Carbohydrates: 5g, Protein: 20g

72. Grilled Beef Tenderloin Skewers with Herb Butter

Grilled Beef Tenderloin Skewers with Herb Butter are a delicious blend of tender and savory. Perfect for a summer cookout, this special recipe with its vibrant herbs and luxurious butter is sure to impress!
Serving: 4
Preparation time: 10 minutes
Ready time: 25 minutes

Ingredients:
- 2 beef tenderloin steaks, cut into 1-inch cubes
- 4 tablespoons butter, melted

- 2 tablespoons finely chopped fresh rosemary
- 2 tablespoons finely chopped fresh thyme
- 2 tablespoons finely chopped fresh parsley
- 1/2 teaspoon kosher salt
- 1/4 teaspoon freshly ground black pepper

Instructions:
1. Heat the grill to medium.
2. Thread the beef cubes onto four skewers, dividing them evenly.
3. In a small bowl, combine the butter, rosemary, thyme, parsley, salt and pepper.
4. Place the skewers on the hot grill and brush with the herb butter. Cook, turning and brushing occasionally with the butter, until the beef is cooked through and lightly charred, about 6 minutes.
5. Serve the skewers with additional herb butter, if desired.

Nutrition Information (per serving): 289 calories, 22 g fat, 10 g carbohydrates, 16 g protein.

73. Beef and Radish Leaf Skewers

Beef and Radish Leaf Skewers
This savory dish features marinated beef and radish leaf skewers seasoned with a delightful blend of spices. It's an easy-to-make favorite for any party or occasion!
Serving: 6-8
Preparation time: 15 minutes
Ready Time: 40 minutes

Ingredients:
- 2 lbs flank steak, cut into cubes
- 2 tablespoons olive oil
- 2 teaspoons sesame oil
- 2 tablespoons soy sauce
- 2 tablespoons rice wine
- 2 tablespoons minced garlic
- 1 tablespoon grated ginger
- 1 teaspoon black pepper

- 2 bunches of green radish leaves
- 6-8 bamboo skewers

Instructions:
1. In a large bowl, mix together the olive oil, sesame oil, soy sauce, rice wine, garlic, ginger, and black pepper.
2. Add the steak cubes and stir to coat. Let marinate for 30 minutes at room temperature.
3. Meanwhile, rinse the radish leaves and trim off any thick stems.
4. Thread the marinated steak cubes and radish leaves onto the skewers.
5. Heat a large skillet over medium-high heat and add the skewers.
6. Cook for about 10 minutes, turning the skewers every few minutes to evenly cook.
7. Serve the skewers with your favorite side dishes.

Nutrition Information:
Calories per serving: 250
Total fat: 10g
Protein: 25g
Carbohydrates: 4g
Sodium: 400mg

74. Mexican-Style Beef Skewers with Salsa Verde

Mexican-Style Beef Skewers with Salsa Verde
Serving: 4
Preparation Time: 10 minutes
Ready Time: 30 minutes

Ingredients:
-1 lb beef sirloin, cut into 1-inch cubes
-2 tablespoons olive oil
-1 teaspoon smoked paprika
-1/2 teaspoon chili powder
-1/2 teaspoon garlic powder
-1/4 teaspoon ground cumin
-Salt and pepper
-2 tomatoes, diced

-1 jalapeno, seeded and diced
-3 cloves garlic, minced
-1/2 cup chopped fresh cilantro
-1/4 cup extra-virgin olive oil
-2 tablespoons lime juice
-Salt and pepper to taste

Instructions:
1. Preheat the oven to 375 degrees F.
2. In a large bowl, combine the beef cubes, olive oil, paprika, chili powder, garlic powder, cumin, salt, and pepper. Toss to combine.
3. Thread the beef cubes onto skewers and place on a lightly greased baking sheet.
4. Bake for 15-20 minutes, or until the beef is cooked through.
5. In the meantime, make the salsa. In a medium bowl, combine the tomatoes, jalapeno, garlic, cilantro, olive oil, lime juice, salt, and pepper.
6. Serve the beef skewers alongside the salsa verde. Enjoy!

Nutrition Information:
Calories: 300 per serving
Fat: 18g
Carbohydrates: 6g
Protein: 23g

75. Beef and Parsnip Skewers

Try these delicious Beef and Parsnip Skewers for your next dinner! The tender steak and sweet parsnips combine in this delectable recipe, sure to please everyone's taste buds.
Serving: 4
Preparation Time: 20 minutes
Ready Time: 30 minutes

Ingredients:
- 2 tablespoons of extra-virgin olive oil
- 1 pound of beef sirloin steak cut into 1-inch cubes
- 2 parsnips, peeled and cut into 1-inch pieces
- 4 wooden or metal skewers

- Salt and pepper to taste

Instructions:
1. Heat the olive oil in a large frying pan over medium-high heat.
2. Add the beef cubes and season with salt and pepper. Cook until the beef is browned on all sides, about 5 minutes.
3. Thread the beef cubes and parsnip pieces onto the skewers, alternating between the two.
4. Heat a grill pan over medium heat and lightly coat with oil.
5. Place the skewers on the grill pan and cook until the beef is cooked through and the parsnips are tender, about 10 minutes.
6. Serve the skewers hot.

Nutrition Information: Per serving: 227 calories; 12.2 g fat; 1.2 g saturated fat; 21 mg cholesterol; 208 mg sodium; 10.1 g carbohydrates; 2.5 g fiber; 27.1 g protein.

76. Greek-Style Beef Skewers with Tirokafteri Sauce

These juicy Greek-style beef skewers are slathered in an ultra-flavorful Tirokafteri sauce, made with feta cheese, tomato paste, chili, garlic, and fresh herbs. The perfect summer BBQ meal or appetizer for any time of year!
Serving: 6-8
Preparation Time: 20 minutes
Ready Time: 45 minutes

Ingredients:
• 2 lbs. lean stewing beef, cut into 1-inch cubes
• 2 garlic cloves, minced
• 2 tbsp. olive oil
• 2 tsp. oregano
• 2 tsp. thyme
• Salt and pepper to taste
For the Tirokafteri sauce:
• ½ cup crumbled feta cheese
• 2 tbsp. tomato paste
• 1 red chili, finely chopped

- 1 garlic clove, minced
- 2 tsp. fresh oregano
- 2 tsp. fresh thyme
- Salt and pepper to taste
- ¼ cup extra-virgin olive oil

Instructions:
1. Preheat the oven to 375°F.
2. Place the beef cubes in a large bowl and add the garlic, olive oil, oregano, thyme, salt, and pepper. Toss to combine and allow to marinate for 15 minutes.
3. In a separate bowl, combine the feta cheese, tomato paste, chili, garlic, oregano, thyme, salt, and pepper.
4. Drizzle with the olive oil and mix to combine.
5. Skewer the beef cubes onto metal or soaked wooden skewers.
6. Place the skewers onto a lightly greased baking sheet and top with the tirokafteri sauce.
7. Bake for 25-30 minutes, or until the beef is cooked through.

Nutrition Information:
Calories: 312
Fat: 17.5 g
Carbohydrates: 3.3 g
Protein: 34.3 g

77. Beef and Brussels Sprouts Kabobs

Beef and Brussels Sprouts Kabobs are a delicious and flavorful way to enjoy the flavors of beef and roasted Brussels sprouts! Marinated in a tangy balsamic mixture then combined with chunks of juicy beef and hearty Brussels sprouts, these kabobs are sure to be a summertime favorite!
Serving: 4
Preparation Time: 10 minutes
Ready Time: 40 minutes

Ingredients:
-1 1/2 pounds beef sirloin steak, cut into 1-inch cubes

-2 1/2 cups Brussels Sprouts, trimmed and halved
-1/4 cup Balsamic vinegar
-2 tablespoons Olive oil
-1/2 teaspoon Salt
-1/4 teaspoon Black pepper
-1/2 teaspoon Garlic powder
-2 teaspoons Dried oregano

Instructions:
1. In a large bowl, combine beef cubes, Brussels Sprouts, and prepared balsamic vinaigrette.
2. Preheat your grill to medium-high heat.
3. Thread the marinated beef and Brussels sprouts onto skewers and place on the preheated grill.
4. Grill the beef and Brussels sprouts kabobs for 12-14 minutes, flipping them once during the cooking process, or until the beef is cooked through with an internal temperature of 160°F.
5. Remove from the grill, season with extra salt and pepper to taste, and enjoy!

Nutrition Information:
Calories: 266, Total Fat: 11 g, Saturated Fat: 3 g, Cholesterol: 69 mg, Sodium: 368 mg, Total Carbohydrates: 6 g, Total Fiber: 2 g, Protein: 29 g.

78. Cajun-Style Beef and Andouille Skewers

This easy-to-make Cajun-Style Beef and Andouille Skewers recipe offers a delicious blend of colorful vegetables, juicy steak, and smoky Andouille sausage! The perfect summer meal to fire up the grill.
Serving: 4
Preparation time: 20 minutes
Ready time: 30 minutes

Ingredients:
• 1 ½ lbs steak (sirloin & sirloin tip, or your favorite cut)
• 2 links Andouille sausage, sliced into ½" thick coins
• ¼ cup chicken broth

- 1 teaspoon Cajun seasoning
- 1 tablespoon garlic, minced
- 1 bell pepper, diced
- 1 red onion, diced
- 8 wooden kebab skewers, soaked in salted water for 30 minutes

Instructions:
1. Cut steak into 1" cubes and place in a medium-sized bowl.
2. Add Cajun seasoning and garlic. Mix gently to make sure all cubes are evenly coated.
3. Place steak, sausage, bell pepper, and red onion onto kebab skewers.
4. Heat outdoor grill to medium-high heat (or alternatively heat a cast iron skillet on stovetop at the same temperature).
5. Place kebabs on grill, cook on each side for approximately 3 minutes for medium-rare steak, or until steak is cooked to your desired doneness.
6. Place chicken broth in skillet and swirl to evenly coat the pan.
7. Place skewered beef and vegetables in skillet with chicken broth and allow to simmer for 4-5 minutes, stirring regularly.
8. Serve warm.

Nutrition Information:
- Calories: 554 kcal
- Total Fat: 34 g
- Saturated Fat: 12 g
- Cholesterol: 103 mg
- Sodium: 506 mg
- Total Carbohydrates: 13 g
- Protein: 41 g

79. Beef and Watermelon Skewers

Beef and Watermelon Skewers
Serving: 4
Preparation Time: 10 minutes
Ready Time: 15 minutes

Ingredients:
- 2 tablespoons olive oil

- 2 tablespoons hoisin sauce
- 2 cloves garlic, minced
- 2 teaspoons grated fresh ginger
- ¼ teaspoon kosher salt
- 12 ounces beef top sirloin, cut into 1-inch cubes
- 2 cups cubed seedless watermelon
- 6 metal skewers, soaked in water for 10 minutes
- 2 tablespoons chopped fresh basil

Instructions:
1. In a medium bowl, whisk together the oil, hoisin sauce, garlic, ginger and salt.
2. Add in the beef cubes and toss to coat. Marinate for 10 minutes.
3. Preheat a grill or grill pan over medium-high heat.
4. Thread beef cubes and watermelon onto skewers, alternating between the two.
5. Grill skewers for 2-3 minutes per side, or until the beef is cooked to your desired doneness.
6. Remove skewers from heat and sprinkle with fresh basil. Serve immediately.

Nutrition Information (per skewer): 180 calories, 10g fat, 5g saturated fat, 435mg sodium, 8g carbohydrate, 1g fiber, 22g protein

80. Beef and Turnip Skewers

Fire up the grill and start making these delicious Beef and Turnip Skewers! These easy skewers are perfect for quick weeknight dinners or entertaining.
Serving: 4
Preparation Time: 10 minutes
Ready Time: 20 minutes

Ingredients:
• 1 lb lean ground beef
• 2 cups peeled and diced turnips
• ¼ teaspoon garlic powder
• ¼ teaspoon onion powder

- 1 teaspoon dried oregano
- ¼ teaspoon paprika
- 1 tablespoon olive oil
- Salt and pepper to taste

Instructions:
1. Preheat the grill and preheat to medium.
2. In a bowl, mix together the ground beef, turnips, garlic powder, onion powder, oregano, paprika, salt, pepper, and olive oil.
3. Once everything is combined, scoop out the beef and turnip mixture and form them into 2 inch patties.
4. Skewer the patties and place the skewers onto the grill.
5. Grill for 8-10 minutes, flipping the skewers half way through, or until the patties are cooked through.
6. Once the patties are cooked, remove them from the grill and serve.

Nutrition Information:
Serving Size: 1 skewer
Calories: 178 kcal
Fat: 9.7 g
Carbohydrates: 4.5 g
Protein: 17.3 g

81. Chimichurri Beef and Potato Skewers

Chimichurri Beef and Potato Skewers – Delicious grilled beef and potato skewers marinated in a flavorful chimichurri sauce.
Serving: 4
Preparation Time: 15 minutes
Ready Time: 20 minutes

Ingredients:
- 2 tablespoons of olive oil
- 1/4 cup of fresh parsley, finely chopped
- 2 cloves garlic, minced
- 1 tablespoons of red wine vinegar
- 1/2 teaspoon of cumin
- Salt and pepper to taste

- 1 onion, diced
- 1 1/2 pounds of beef sirloin, cubed
- 5 large Yukon gold potatoes, cut into 1-inch cubes
- 8 wooden skewers

Instructions:
1. In a small bowl, whisk together olive oil, parsley, garlic, red wine vinegar, and cumin. Season with salt and pepper to taste.
2. Place the beef cubes, diced onion, and potato cubes in a large bowl. Pour the chimichurri sauce over the top and toss until everything is evenly coated.
3. Preheat your grill to medium-high heat.
4. Skewer the beef and potatoes, alternating between both. Place the skewers on the hot grill grates and cook for 5-7 minutes per side, or until the beef is cooked through and the potatoes are tender.
5. Once the skewers are cooked through, remove from the heat and serve.

Nutrition Information (Per Serving):
Calorie: 313
Total Fat: 11g
Sodium: 53mg
Carbohydrate: 25g
Protein: 27g

82. Beef and Green Papaya Skewers

Beef and Green Papaya Skewers
Serving: 4
Preparation Time: 10 minutes
Ready Time: 15 minutes

Ingredients:
- 1 large green papaya, cut into 2-inch cubes
- 1 lb. lean sirloin steak, cut into 1-inch cubes
- 2 tbsp. canola oil
- 1 tsp. ground black pepper
- 1 tsp. chili powder

- 2 cloves garlic, minced
- 2 tbsp. fish sauce

Instructions:
1. Preheat your grill to medium-high heat.
2. In a large bowl, combine the green papaya cubes, sirloin cubes, oil, ground pepper, chili powder, garlic, and fish sauce. Mix until all the cubes are evenly coated.
3. Skewer the papaya and beef cubes onto separate skewers.
4. Place the skewers on the preheated grill and cook for 5-8 minutes, turning occasionally, until chicken is cooked through and papaya is golden and tender.
5. Remove from heat and serve.

Nutrition Information:
Calories: 266 kcal, Total Fat: 14 g, Saturated Fat: 4 g, Cholesterol: 65 mg, Sodium: 209 mg, Carbohydrates: 7 g, Fiber: 2 g, Protein: 27 g

83. Smoky Paprika Beef Skewers

These Smoky Paprika Beef Skewers are a great way to bring some delicious smoked flavor to your next barbeque. Seared with a homemade smoky paprika marinade, these beef skewers are sure to be a hit.
Serving: 6
Preparation Time: 15 minutes
Ready Time: 2 hours

Ingredients:
• 750g beef steak, cut into thin strips
• 2 tsp smoked paprika
• 2 tbsp olive oil
• 1 lemon, juice only
• 2 cloves garlic, minced
• 1 tsp sea salt
• ½ tsp ground black pepper

Instructions:

1. In a large bowl, combine the smoked paprika, olive oil, lemon juice, garlic, sea salt and black pepper and mix together to form a marinade.
2. Add the beef slices to the bowl and mix to evenly coat all the pieces in the marinade.
3. Let the beef marinade for a minimum of 1 hour in the fridge.
4. Preheat your BBQ to a medium heat.
5. Thread the beef slices onto skewers and place onto the BBQ. Cook for 5-7 minutes on each side, or until the beef is cooked to your liking.
6. Serve with your favorite sides.

Nutrition Information: Per serving (175g) – Calories 301, Fat 9g, Carbohydrates 0g, Protein 49g

84. Beef and Jicama Skewers

Enjoy these delicious Asian-style Beef and Jicama Skewers, perfect for any type of gathering or meal.
Serving: Makes 6 skewers
Preparation Time: 10 minutes
Ready Time: 15 minutes

Ingredients:
- 1 small jicama, cubed
- 1 lb beef steak, cut into 1-inch cubes
- 2 teaspoons soy sauce
- 1 teaspoon toasted sesame oil
- 2 cloves garlic, minced
- 2 tablespoons fresh ginger, grated
- 1/2 teaspoon ground black pepper
- 12 skewers

Instructions:
1. Preheat oven to 400°F.
2. In a medium bowl, combine the beef cubes, soy sauce, sesame oil, garlic, ginger, and pepper.
3. Thread the beef and jicama cubes onto the skewers, leaving a little bit of space between each piece.

4. Place the skewers on a greased baking sheet and bake for 10-15 minutes, or until the beef is cooked to your desired doneness.

Nutrition Information: Per Skewer: 180 calories, 9g fat, 2g carbohydrates, 22g protein

85. Chinese-Style Beef and Scallion Skewers

Chinese-Style Beef and Scallion Skewers
Serving: 4
Preparation time: 30 minutes
Ready time: 30 minutes

Ingredients:
• 1 pound flank steak, cut into 1/2-inch cubes
• 2 tablespoons soy sauce
• 2 tablespoons Chinese black vinegar
• 1 tablespoon sesame oil
• 1 teaspoon five-spice powder
• 1 tablespoon vegetable oil
• 2 scallions, finely chopped
• Salt

Instructions:
1. In a medium bowl, combine the flank steak, soy sauce, vinegar, sesame oil and five-spice powder. Mix well to combine and let marinate at least 30 minutes, up to an hour.
2. Heat a cast iron griddle, skillet or wok over high heat. When hot, add the vegetable oil. When the oil is hot, add the beef cubes and the scallions. Cook for 1-2 minutes or until the beef is cooked through.
3. Transfer the beef skewers to a platter and season with salt. Serve.

Nutrition Information:
Calories: 266 kcal, Carbohydrates: 2 g, Protein: 25 g,Fat: 17 g, Sodium: 863 mg, Potassium: 376 mg, Sugar: 1 g, Vitamin C: 1 mg, Calcium: 33 mg, Iron: 2 mg

Beef and Kohlrabi Leaf Skewers: A unique and flavourful take on the traditional skewer, these beef and kohlrabi leaf skewers are sure to tantalise the taste buds! With a quick prep time and delectable end result, this dish is ideal for any gathering.
Serving: 4
Preparation Time: 15 minutes
Ready Time: 30 minutes

Ingredients:
- 500g lean beef mince
- 2 tablespoons vegetable oil
- 4 kohlrabi leaves
- 2 tablespoons finely chopped fresh mint leaves
- 1 teaspoon ground cumin

Instructions:
1. In a large bowl, combine the beef mince, oil, mint leaves, and cumin. Mix together until well combined.
2. Take a kohlrabi leaf and place a handful of the beef mince mixture onto the leaf. Roll or fold the leaf around the beef mince, ensuring the beef mixture is sealed inside the leaf. Repeat with the remaining leaves and beef mixture.
3. Preheat the grill to medium-high heat. Place the beef and kohlrabi leaf skewers onto the grill and cook for approximately 10 to 15 minutes, turning the skewers occasionally to ensure even cooking.
4. Once the beef skewers have cooked through, remove from the heat and serve immediately.

Nutrition Information:
Per Serving: Calories 268, Protein 25.5g, Total Fat 15.5g, Carbohydrates 4g, Cholesterol 59mg, Sodium 84mg

Lemon Herb Beef Skewers are an easy and delicious way to add some flavor to your barbecue. These skewered beef cubes are marinated in a

zesty lemon and herb sauce, then cooked on the grill for a juicy and flavorful meal.
Serving: 6-7 skewers
Preparation Time: 10 minutes
Ready Time: 15 minutes

Ingredients:
- 1 lb beef cubes
- 2 tablespoons lemon juice
- 1 tablespoon olive oil
- 2 teaspoons dried oregano
- 1 teaspoon garlic powder
- 1 teaspoon dried thyme
- Salt and pepper, to taste

Instructions:
1. Start by marinating the beef cubes. Combine the lemon juice, olive oil, oregano, garlic powder, thyme, salt, and pepper in a bowl and mix together until combined.
2. Add the beef cubes to the marinade and toss them until each cube is fully coated. Cover the bowl and refrigerate for at least 1 hour, or overnight.
3. To cook the skewers, preheat a grill or grill pan to medium-high heat.
4. Once the grill is hot, remove the beef cubes from the marinade and thread them onto skewers.
5. Grill the skewers for 3-4 minutes per side, or until cooked to your desired doneness.
6. Serve the Lemon Herb Beef Skewers warm.

Nutrition Information:
Serving Size: 1 skewer
Calories: 140 | Total Fat: 8g | Saturated Fat: 3g | Total Carbohydrates: 0g | Protein: 18g

88. Beef and Cabbage Leaf Skewers

Beef and Cabbage Leaf Skewers is a flavorful and healthy dish that makes the perfect appetizer or main course. Featuring marinated beef skewers wrapped in cabbage leaves and coated in a delicious sauce, these skewers get extra crunch from skewered vegetables.

Serving: 4
Preparation Time: 15 minutes
Ready Time: 55 minutes

Ingredients:
- 1 lb Ground Beef
- 2 cloves Garlic, minced
- 2 tablespoons Soy Sauce
- 1 teaspoon Red Pepper Flakes
- 2 tablespoons Sesame Oil
- 2 teaspoons Brown Sugar
- 16 Cabbage Leaves
- 4 Skewers
- 1 Red Bell Pepper, sliced
- 1 Orange Bell Pepper, sliced
- 4 Green Onions, diced
- Salt and Pepper to taste

Instructions:
1. Preheat oven to 350 degrees
2. In a large bowl, combine Ground Beef, Garlic, Soy Sauce, Red Pepper Flakes, Sesame Oil, and Brown Sugar. Mix until all Ingredients are evenly incorporated.
3. Take one-quarter of the mixture and place in the center of one cabbage leaf. Fold the sides of the leaf over the mixture and skewer the cabbage wrap to secure it with a skewer. Repeat this process for the remaining mixture.
4. Arrange the skewers on a baking sheet and top with the Bell Peppers and Green Onions. Sprinkle with Salt and Pepper to taste.
5. Bake in preheated oven for 40 minutes.
6. Serve warm. Enjoy!

Nutrition Information:
Calories: 208 kcal; Fat: 15.4g; Carbohydrates: 3.4g; Protein: 15.7g; Cholesterol: 43.4mg; Sodium: 419.4mg; Potassium: 251.1mg; Fiber: 0.7g; Sugar: 1.8g

89. BBQ Beef and Pickle Skewers

BBQ Beef and Pickle Skewers
Serving: Makes 4 skewers
Preparation Time: 10 minutes
Ready Time: 10 minutes

Ingredients:
- 4 bamboo skewers
- ½ lb. thinly sliced ribeye steak
- 4 garlic cloves, finely grated
- 2 tablespoons olive oil
- 2 tablespoons Worcestershire sauce
- Freshly ground black pepper, to taste
- 4 dill pickles, each cut into 8 pieces

Instructions:
1. Soak the bamboo skewers in water for at least 10 minutes.
2. In a medium bowl, combine the steak, garlic, olive oil, Worcestershire sauce, and black pepper. Mix until everything is well combined.
3. Place the steak onto the skewers along with the pickles.
4. Heat a non-stick skillet over medium-high heat.
5. Place the skewers onto the skillet and cook each side for about 4 minutes or until the steak is cooked through.
6. Serve and enjoy.

Nutrition Information:
Calories: 150; Total Fat: 7g; Cholesterol: 47mg; Sodium: 311mg; Total Carbohydrates: 2g; Protein: 15g.

90. Korean-Style Beef Skewers with Kimchi

These flavorful Korean-Style Beef Skewers with Kimchi make for the ultimate party food or BBQ fare. The combination of sweet, spicy, and savory is oh so satisfying.
Serving: 4-6
Preparation Time: 20 minutes
Ready Time: 30 minutes

Ingredients:
- 2 cloves garlic, minced
- 2 tablespoons soy sauce
- 1 tablespoon sweet chili sauce
- 2 tablespoons mirin
- 1 lb. sirloin steak, sliced into thin strips
- 2 tablespoons toasted sesame oil
- 2 cups kimchi

Instructions:
1. In a medium bowl, combine the garlic, soy sauce, sweet chili sauce, and mirin. Add the steak strips, and mix until they are evenly coated.
2. Heat a large skillet over medium heat, and add the sesame oil. Once hot, add the steak strips to the skillet, and cook for 1-2 minutes on each side.
3. Preheat the grill to medium-high heat. Skewer the steak onto metal skewers.
4. Grill the skewers for 2 minutes. Flip over the skewers, and cook for an additional 2 minutes.
5. Once the steak is cooked, remove from the skewers and place on a plate. Serve with kimchi.

Nutrition Information: Per serving (Serving size: 1 skewer): Calories: 168 kcal, Protein: 15 g, Fat: 9 g, Cholesterol: 46 mg, Sodium: 707 mg, Carbohydrates: 5 g, Fiber: 0.5 g

91. Beef and Spring Onion Skewers

Beef and Spring Onion Skewers - A delightful Asian-inspired version of a classic beef kebab, these skewers are bursting with flavor - a mix of ground beef, spring onions, garlic, soy sauce, and sesame oil to create a flavor sensation. Serve with sticky white rice or a side of Asian vegetables for a meal the entire family will love.
Serving: 4
Preparation Time: 10 mins
Ready Time: 15 mins

Ingredients:
- 1 lb. ground beef
- 2 cloves garlic, minced
- 2 spring onions, chopped
- 2 tablespoons soy sauce
- 1 tablespoon sesame oil
- 4 skewers

Instructions:
1. Preheat a grill to medium-high heat and lightly oil the grate with vegetable oil.
2. In a large bowl, combine the ground beef, garlic, spring onions, soy sauce and sesame oil.
3. Mix together until all of the Ingredients are evenly distributed.
4. Divide the mixture into four even portions.
5. Form each portion into a cylinder shape, and place each cylinder onto a skewer.
6. Place the skewers onto the grill, and cook for 5-7 minutes per side, until the beef is cooked through.
7. Serve the skewers with sticky white rice or Asian vegetables, and enjoy.

Nutrition Information:
Calories: 294 kcal, Carbohydrates: 5 g, Protein: 26 g, Fat: 17 g, Saturated Fat: 6 g, Cholesterol: 82 mg, Sodium: 599 mg, Potassium: 492 mg, Fiber: 1 g, Sugar: 2 g, Vitamin A: 164 IU, Vitamin C: 3 mg, Calcium: 22 mg, Iron: 2 mg

92. Indonesian-Style Beef Satay Skewers with Peanut Sauce

Indonesian-Style Beef Satay Skewers with Peanut Sauce is a delicious and flavorful dish that will bring a delightfully exotic twist to any meal. This recipe combines marinated beef strips, skewered and grilled, with a flavorful peanut sauce.
Serving: Serves 4
Preparation Time: 10 minutes
Ready Time: 33 minutes

Ingredients:
- 1 ½ lbs sirloin steak, cut into thin strips
- 1 Tbsp oil or melted coconut oil
- 1 clove garlic, finely chopped
- 2 tsp finely grated fresh ginger
- 2 tsp curry powder
- 2 Tbsp light soy sauce
- 2 Tbsp honey
- 2 Tbsp vegetable oil
- 2 Tbsp white wine vinegar
- ¼ cup crunchy peanut butter
- 2 Tbsp water
- 2 Tbsp chopped fresh cilantro

Instructions:
1. Combine the beef strips, oil, garlic, ginger, curry powder, soy sauce, honey, vegetable oil, and vinegar in a medium bowl and mix until the beef is fully coated in the mixture.
2. Thread the beef strips onto metal skewers.
3. Heat a grill or skillet to medium-high heat and place the skewers on the grill or skillet, cooking until the beef is browned and cooked through, about 5 minutes.
4. Meanwhile, in a small bowl, mix together the peanut butter, water, and cilantro until smooth.
5. Serve the skewers hot with the peanut sauce on the side.

Nutrition Information: Calories: 308, Total Fat: 17.3 g, Saturated Fat: 4.7 g, Trans Fat: 0.1 g, Cholesterol: 59.7 mg, Sodium: 480.2 mg, Carbohydrates: 11.9 g, Fiber: 1.1 g, Sugar: 8.3 g, Protein: 25.3g

93. Beef and Parsley Root Skewers

Tired of the same old grilled skewers? Try this new take on a classic with these delicious beef and parsley root skewers, a blend of beef and flavorful veggies.
Serving: 4
Preparation Time: 30 minutes
Ready Time: 1 hour

Ingredients:
1 lb beef stew meat, cut into cubes
1 medium parsley root, cut into 2" cubes
2 tablespoons olive oil
1 tablespoon fresh rosemary
Salt and pepper to taste

Instructions:
1. Preheat the grill to medium-high heat.
2. In a large bowl, combine the beef, parsley root, olive oil, rosemary, salt and pepper. Mix until the Ingredients are well-combined.
3. Shape the mixture into four even-sized skewers.
4. Place the skewers on the preheated grill and cook for 8 minutes, flipping once halfway through until the beef and parsley root are cooked through and lightly charred.
5. Serve and enjoy.

Nutrition Information: 434 calories, 21g fat, 33g protein, 18g carbohydrates, 5.2g fiber, 322mg sodium

94. Italian-Style Beef and Radicchio Skewers with Balsamic Glaze

These delicious Italian-style beef and radicchio skewers with a balsamic glaze are full of zesty flavor.
Serving: 4-6
Preparation time: 20 minutes
Ready time: 8 hours (includes marinating time)

Ingredients:
• 1/4 cup balsamic vinegar
• 2 tablespoons olive oil
• 2 cloves garlic, minced
• 1 teaspoon Italian seasoning
• Salt and pepper, to taste
• 1 ½ pound lean beef sirloin, cut into 1-inch cubes
• ½ head of radicchio, cut into 1-inch pieces

• 8 wooden or metal skewers

Instructions:
1. In a large bowl, mix together balsamic vinegar, olive oil, garlic, Italian seasoning, salt and pepper.
2. Add the cubed beef and mix until well combined. Cover and marinate for at least 8 hours in the refrigerator.
3. Preheat your grill or grill pan to medium-high heat.
4. Thread the beef cubes and radicchio onto the skewers, alternating pieces.
5. Grill skewers for 4-5 minutes, flipping once, until the beef is cooked to your desired doneness.
6. Drizzle the balsamic glaze over the skewers before serving.

Nutrition Information:
Calories: 282 kcal, Carbohydrates: 6 g, Protein: 22 g, Fat: 19 g, Saturated Fat: 6 g, Cholesterol: 63 mg, Sodium: 36 mg, Potassium: 427 mg, Fiber: 1 g, Sugar: 4 g, Vitamin A: 25 IU, Vitamin C: 3 mg, Calcium: 35 mg, Iron: 2 mg

95. Beef and Bok Choy Skewers

Beef and Bok Choy Skewers - An easy and delicious Asian-inspired meal that can be prepared in no time!
Serving: 4
Preparation time: 15 minutes
Ready time: 25 minutes

Ingredients:
- 1 lb. top sirloin beef, cut into 1-inch cubes
- 1 head of bok choy, leaves separated and ends trimmed
- 2 cloves minced garlic
- 2 teaspoons minced fresh ginger
- 4 tablespoons soy sauce
- 2 tablespoons vegetable oil
- 4-6 wooden skewers

Instructions:

1. Preheat the grill to medium-high heat.
2. In a medium bowl, combine the soy sauce, garlic, ginger, and vegetable oil. Mix together and add the cubed beef to the marinade. Set aside.
3. Thread 4-6 cubes of beef onto each skewer, alternating between beef and bok choy leaves.
4. Grill the skewers over medium-high heat for 5-6 minutes per side, or until the beef is cooked to your preference.
5. Serve hot.

Nutrition Information (per serving):
Calories: 253
Total fat: 11g
Sodium: 647mg
Carbohydrates: 4g
Protein: 31g

96. Turkish-Style Beef Skewers with Yogurt Sauce

These Turkish-Style Beef Skewers with Yogurt Sauce are an easy and flavorful dinner recipe that everyone will love! Succulent beef skewers are marinated with flavorful seasonings, grilled to perfection, then served with a creamy and tangy yogurt sauce.
Serving: 4-6
Preparation Time: 15 minutes
Ready Time: 15 minutes

Ingredients:
- 1 lb. lean beef top sirloin, cut into 1 1/2-inch cubes
- 2 tablespoons olive oil
- 1 tablespoon lemon juice
- 1 teaspoon ground cumin
- 1 teaspoon garlic powder
- 1 teaspoon paprika
- 1/4 teaspoon salt
- 1/4 teaspoon black pepper
- 1/2 cup plain Greek yogurt
- 2 tablespoons chopped fresh parsley
- 2 teaspoons minced garlic

- 1/4 teaspoon salt

Instructions:
1. In a medium bowl combine the olive oil, lemon juice, cumin, garlic powder, paprika, salt, and pepper. Add the beef cubes and toss to coat. Thread the cubes onto 6-8 skewers.
2. Preheat a grill pan over medium-high heat. Lightly grease the pan with cooking spray then add the skewers. Grill for 2-3 minutes per side or until the beef is cooked to desired doneness.
3. To make the yogurt sauce, combine the yogurt, parsley, garlic, and salt in a small bowl. Serve the beef skewers with the yogurt sauce.

Nutrition Information (per serving):
Calories: 351, Fat: 20g, Saturated Fat: 5g, Cholesterol: 79mg, Sodium: 343mg, Carbohydrates: 5g, Fiber: 1g, Sugar: 2g, Protein: 35g

97. Beef and Endive Skewers

Beef and Endive Skewers
This recipe is a great way to pack in some protein and vitamins all in one easy dish. Savory beef, tart endive, and a kick from the garlic and paprika create a wonderful flavor combination that your guests will love. Serve this as an appetizer or main dish, and enjoy!
Serving: 8
Preparation Time: 15 minutes
Ready Time: 30 minutes

Ingredients:
• 1 pound sirloin steak, cut into 2-inch cubes
• 8 small endives, leaves separated
• 2 tablespoons olive oil
• 1 clove garlic, minced
• 1 teaspoon paprika
• 1 teaspoon coarse sea salt
• 1 teaspoon freshly ground black pepper

Instructions:
1. Preheat oven to 375°F.

2. Toss steak cubes with olive oil, garlic, paprika, salt and pepper until evenly coated.

3. Thread a steak cube and endive leaf onto each skewer, alternating the two until skewer is full.

4. Place skewers onto a parchment-lined baking sheet. Bake for 15 minutes or until steak is cooked to desired doneness.

Nutrition Information:
• Calories: 170 kcal
• Protein: 23g
• Total fat: 8g
• Carbohydrates: 3g
• Fiber: 1g
• Sodium: 393mg

98. Beer-Marinated Beef Skewers with Mustard Sauce

Beer-Marinated Beef Skewers with Mustard Sauce
This flavorful dish is a delicious and easy way to make great use of marinating beef in beer. The mustard sauce is tangy and adds a delicious flavor to the tender beef. Serve these skewers with a side of roasted potatoes, grilled vegetables, and crusty bread for a scrumptious meal.
Serving: 8
Preparation: 15 minutes
Ready: 4 hours

Ingredients:
- 2 pounds of beef tenderloin, sliced into 1-2 inch cubes
- 1 bottle of beer
- 2 tablespoons of Worcestershire sauce
- 2 garlic cloves, minced
- 1 teaspoon of salt
- ½ teaspoon of black pepper
- 2 tablespoons of olive oil
- 2 tablespoons of Dijon mustard
- 2 tablespoons of honey
- 2 tablespoons of white wine vinegar

Instructions:
1. In a large bowl, combine the beef, beer, Worcestershire sauce, garlic, salt, and pepper. Mix well and set aside for at least 2 hours.
2. Preheat a grill or grill pan to medium-high heat and lightly oil the surface.
3. Thread the beef cubes onto skewers and brush with olive oil. Grill for 4-5 minutes on each side, or until cooked to desired doneness.
4. In a small bowl, whisk together the mustard, honey, and white wine vinegar.
5. Serve the beef skewers with the mustard sauce.

Nutrition Information:
Serving Size: 1 Skewer (4 oz)
Calories: 250
Total Fat: 11g
Saturated Fat: 4g
Cholesterol: 65mg
Sodium: 530mg
Carbohydrates: 10g
Protein: 24g

CONCLUSION

Skewered Delights: 98 Flavorful Beef BBQ and Grilled Kabobs is a cookbook that allows meat-lovers to explore the diverse and delicious world of kabobs. This cookbook is a wonderful guide for individuals who love beef and want to add some exciting new flavors to their barbecuing or grilling routine. With 98 different kabob recipes, the book offers a wide range of ideas and inspirations, from classic dishes to modern twists on traditional favorites.

The book is easy to navigate and each recipe is accompanied by a beautiful photograph so that readers can see what they are cooking. From fruity, tropical-inspired kabobs to spicy and smoky dishes, Skewered Delights provides a full range of meaty flavor sensations. Some of the most impressive recipes include the Teriyaki-Glazed Beef and Pineapple Skewers, the Mediterranean Beef Kabobs with Tzatziki Sauce, and the Smoky Chipotle Beef Skewers.

Despite the many recipes available in Skewered Delights, the book is also quite accessible to beginners. Author Lisa Lotts offers helpful tips on preparing and cooking each dish, which is essential for any less experienced cook. The recipes themselves are also clear and easy to follow, ensuring each dish is made perfectly.

Overall, Skewered Delights is an ideal cookbook for anyone who wants to experiment with grilling or barbecuing beef. It offers a wealth of information on different cuts of meat, seasonal ingredients, and marinades to use for kabob cooking. Moreover, the variety of recipes and flavors offered encourage people to try new combinations and experiment with their own unique culinary creations.

As a final note, Skewered Delights: 98 Flavorful Beef BBQ and Grilled Kabobs serves as a great tool to help people explore and broaden their palate. The author's passion for kabobs is evident in every page, and her knowledge and creativity make this cookbook a valuable asset to any kitchen. Whether you are a barbecue master or a beginner cook, Skewered Delights is an excellent cookbook that is sure to impress and satisfy all flavor cravings.

Made in the USA
Las Vegas, NV
30 June 2024

91715486R00059